Ancient India's Royal Queen Mathematics

Dinkar G. Wagle

KALPAZ

ISBN: 978-93-86397-86-7

First Published, 2018

Published by

Kalpaz Publications
C-30, Satyawati Nagar,
Delhi – 110052
E-mail: kalpaz@hotmail.com
Ph.: 9212142040

Printed at: G. Print Process, Delhi

Contents

Preface

Symbols are amazing creations. They rule our lives. When we overestimate their power, we suffer and when we underestimate their power, we suffer. Just what is a symbol? Why are they so important to us?

Symbols are all we have to communicate with one another, to share our ideas and feelings. Why every word you use is a symbol and nothing more and nothing less. Much art deals with symbols, ultimately becomes symbolic. Enjoy the symbols around you and learn how to use them and life will be that much more worthwhile.

The origin of symbols more than 125, 000 years ago when the Ethiopians Cushites migrated to India and used these symbols extensively for communication. The knowledge of symbols comes from cuneiforms and hieroglyphs found in Sumer, Mesopotamia and Egypt respectively. From the excavations, Indus Valley symbols traveled to Persia and Greece. The ancient Indian as well as the Middle Eastern culture is based on symbols.

Myths

Writing is one of the most important inventions ever made by human beings. In putting spoken language into visible material form, people could for the first time, store information and transmit it across time and space. Writing was also invented India.

Two common, opposing attitudes exist towards Ancient Indian knowledge of myths. One view regards the Indians with superstitions reverence as having knowledge of cosmic mysteries and as superhuman geniuses. The other attitude, inspired by optimistic beliefs in human progress, considers reliance on ancient knowledge. Out of this came the origin of myth and mythologies. This was simply because truth and falsity is found in both attitudes in the Ancient World history.

Some 5000 years ago, the India's rishis (sages) of the Vedic age propounded three fundamental privileges of human knowledge: Lead from darkness to light, lead from falsehood to Truth and lead from mortality to immortality. The three fundamentals, in turn, were aimed at the scientific inquiry. First, Energy and light (Jyoti) represent the basic support of life. Second, the Search for Truth is developed through logical reasoning and philosophical studies. Third, the search for immortality comes through investigations of medicine, agriculture etc.

All these three elements are very well described in Indian mythological stories which later spread to Egypt, Persian and Greece.

Mythologies are traditional narratives in which events are described as deeds of gods, heroes or other superhuman beings., that is events attributed so causes not acceptable in historical explanation . They are at the same time, or body of popular lore in which the worldview and moral outlook of a group or tradition are embodied. Ancient India religious traditions are extraordinary, rich in myths and they have occupied a central position in religious literature. Myths, because of their involvement with the ritual process, either as explanations or as a corollary, are also part of the actual functioning of the religious system, particularly, in Hinduism.

Historians have always been drawn to the study of Mythology ever since history of religion has been in existence. Just as there are many meanings in a myth, so are there many interpretations.

This book describes the original Indian myths and mythological stories in Greek literature with Greek names.

MYTHOLOGY IS THE SOUL OF THE SOCIETY

I have come to a tentative conclusion that Mythology is the soul of the society. Religion, history, science and culture etc. play secondary roles. The classical purpose is best defined as bringing Man into union with the whole of the society, for Man is only a fraction of the Whole; his identity is defined in the body of the society. The moral and archetypal lessons conveyed through the Myth transmit a sustaining and time less form that both teaches and serves to bind the society closer. Society, in this sense, functions unilaterally as one "Mythological Instructed Community"

Let us begin our journey into the fascinating World of myths, mythology and history. What exactly are the myths? How have they shaped history and culture? What hidden truths lie inside myths and history which have not been covered as yet? The most important question is what role does mythology play in history or vice versa? Similarly, what role does mythology plays in culture, as well as religion of that country?

Introduction

My interest in the subject started about four years ago when I was teaching a mathematics course in a college. The book I used had two chapters on Fibonacci and his mathematical contributions. He introduced our present numerical system (11-12 century) in Europe and secondly, the famous Fibonacci numbers and indices. At the end of the two chapters, a biographical note stated that Fibonacci as a boy was very fond of the colors developed in various flowers and discovered the irregular pattern the colors were displayed when the flowers were in full bloom. Then about a couple of months ago, I was reading financial analysis on global economy when I saw Fibonacci indices were used. This aroused my curiosity and I did some research on Fibonacci and his work.

To my surprise, almost all the work reported by Fibonacci was not his own. When he was 14, he went to Algeria with his father who was the Count of Pisa. There, the young man met an Egyptian mathematician who had just returned to Egypt from India where he studied mathematics for 15 years.

The Egyptian learned of the Indian numerical system which Fibonacci thought was much simpler and effective then the Roman numerical system used in Europe at that time. Secondly, he also learned the origin of the Fibonacci numbers in India developed by a well-known mathematician called Bhaskara who had developed those numbers in his astronomical studies. On return to Italy, Fibonacci introduced these new developments in his published work called Libber Abaci. The popularity of the Indian numbers system was so vast that the entire credit was given to Fibonacci (Ref.1&4). The incidence prompted me to do some more research on the history of Indian mathematics. This is a very big and complicated subject and I do not understand the advanced mathematics to appreciate the subject properly and therefore, I relied on some expert guidance in this article. Five references have been provided for further work. Following is my brief research on ancient Indian mathematics.

Chapter - 1

Redressing the Distortion of the Historical Role of Indian Mathematics

Mathematics has long been considered an invention of European scholars. The contributions from non-European countries were severely neglected. Worse still, numerous key mathematical developments have been wrongly attributed to scholars of European origin. The study of mathematics has long been characterized by a preferential attitude towards Europeans and by omitting real contributions made by non-European countries. This attitude needs to be changed. The recent study shows that the credit owed by the West to other civilizations and particularly to India on the subject of mathematics goes back at least 5000 years.

Introduction

My interest in the subject started about four years ago when I was teaching a mathematics course in a college. The book I used had two chapters on Fibonacci and his mathematical contributions. He introduced our present numerical system (11-12 century) in Europe and secondly, the famous Fibonacci numbers and indices. At the end of the two chapters, a biographical note stated that Fibonacci as a boy was very fond of the colors developed in various flowers and discovered the irregular pattern the colors were displayed when the flowers were in full bloom. Then about a couple of months ago, I was reading financial analysis on global economy when I saw Fibonacci indices were used. This aroused my curiosity and I did some research on Fibonacci and his work.

To my surprise, almost all the work reported by Fibonacci was not his own. When he was 14, he went to Algeria with his father who was the Count of Pisa. There, the young man met an Egyptian mathematician who had just returned to Egypt from India where he studied mathematics for 15 years.

The Egyptian learned of the Indian numerical system which Fibonacci thought was much simpler and effective then the Roman numerical system used in Europe at that time. Secondly, he also learned the origin of the Fibonacci numbers in India developed by a well-known mathematician called Bhaskara2 who had developed those numbers in his astronomical studies. On return to Italy, Fibonacci introduced these new developments in his published work called Libber Abaci. The popularity of the Indian numbers system was so vast that the entire credit was given to Fibonacci (Ref.1&4). The incidence prompted me to do some more research on the history of Indian mathematics. This is a very big and complicated subject and I do not understand the advanced mathematics to appreciate the subject properly and therefore, I relied on some expert guidance in this article. Five references have been provided for further work. Following is my brief research on ancient Indian mathematics.

The History of Indian Mathematics

The entire history can be divided into three main categories:

1. 4000 B.C. to 1500A.D. Indus (Vedic) Civilization
2. 1400 A.D. to 1600 A.D. Muslim Invasion. No new mathematical developments.
3. 1400 A.D. to 1800 A.D. The so called Kerala Mathematics.

Part 1: Indus Civilization 4000B.C. to 1500 A.D. (Ref. 1&2)

In the Vedic period (4000B.C. -1000B.C.), records of mathematical activities are mostly found in the Vedictexts associated with ritual activities. Arithmetic operations (GANIT) i.e., addition, subtraction, multiplication and division, fraction, squares, cubes and roots are enumerated in Narad Vishnu Purana (2000B.C.).

During the excavation of Mohan-jo-daro and Harappa, a much more detailed account was discovered and it included:

(a) Concept of pi (value of 3.142)
(b) Infinite series of expansion.
(c) Trigonometric expansion.
(d) Decimal numeration.
(e) Place value system that allowed Mathematics to be developed in ways that would not

Been possible otherwise.

According to Europeans, the basic chronology of the history of mathematics is quite different. Their history stated that the mathematics is the invention of the Greeks whose work had contributed up to the middle of 500B.C. Following which there was a period of almost 1000 years when no significant work was carried out until the European Renaissance Period which coincided with the reawakening of the learning and culture in Europe which followed the dark ages.

Greece → Renaissance Period → Europe Of Modern Ages

Some European historians made some concessions, acknowledging the work of Egyptians, Babylonians and Indians mathematicians. (Ref. 1 & 4)

GREECE → EUROPE

↓ \ / ↓

India → Arabic → Babylonia → Egypt

The references to non-Europeans were purposely not clear and generally concluded that they were merely reconstruction of the great Greek Works. Indian mathematicians were considered the custodians of the Greek knowledge (Ref.4). A French historian (P. Duhem 1965) stated: "Arabic science only reproduced the teachings from the Greek science". Another French historian (G. Sartan 1927) stated: "one could almost omit Hindu and Chinese developments in mathematics".

Only in the last 20 years, a new chronology of the history of mathematics is being written and it appears the knowledge of Indian mathematicians was spreading faster through the Asian continent and then to Greece and Spain. A new sequence of the spread of mathematics is considered as:

India → Baghdad

↓ ↕

Babylonia → China → Egypt → Greece → Europe

There were a lot of interactions between different countries by way of sea and land. The knowledge of mathematics spread from India to other countries over a number of years.

Philosophy and Mathematics in India

Philosophical doctrines had a profound influence on the development of mathematical concepts and formulations. In the religious tradition, space and time were considered limitless in Jain cosmology. This led to a deep interest in very large numbers and definition of infinite numbers. The Jain mathematicians recognized five different types of infinities: infinity in one direction, in two directions, in area, infinite everywhere and perpetually infinite. Permutations and combinations are listed in BhagavadSutras (3 B.C.).

A particularly important development in the history of Indian Science that had profound impact was the work by Panini (6 B.C.). Mr. Joseph (Ref.5) argues that the algebraic nature of Indian mathematics arises as a consequence of the Sanskrit language.

Mathematics in the service of religion (Ref. 2 & 3)

In the Hindu religion, there are four Vedas: the Rig Veda, the Sama Veda, the Yajur Veda and The AtharvaVeda .These four Vedas form the primary texts of Hinduism and they also had a vast influence on Buddhism, Jainism and Sikh religions. Some chronological confusion exists with regards to the appearance of Vedic religion. G.Joseph (Ref. 5) states 1500B.C.as the forming of the Hindu religion and civilization and the recording of the Vedas, Vedangas and later Sulbasutras. In the Vedic tradition, there was a need to determine the exact time of the religious ceremonies and the accurate construction of the altars that led to the development of astronomy and geometry. Much of the mathematics contained within the Vedas is found in the works called Vedantas, of which there are six. As a result, many rules and development of geometry are found in the Vedic works which include:

(a) Use of geometric shapes including triangles, squares, trapezoid and circles.

(b) Equivalence through numbers and areas.

(c) Early forms of Pythagorean Theorem

(d) Estimation of the value of pi (Π)

In Satpatha Brahmana, three definitions of pi are given:

(a) 25/8 = 3.125

(b) 900/289 =3.1144685

(a) 1156/361= 3.202216

(b)

The calculations in astronomy led to:

(c) 339/108= 3.1389

(d)

Also found in the Vedic works:

(a) Four arithmetic operators i.e., addition, subtraction, multiplication and division

(b) Definition of Zero

(c) Prime numbers

In the Vedic works, that the term GANITA which literally means the science of calculation was mentioned throughout the texts.

SULBA SUTRAS (800 B.C. – 200 B.C.)

The developments include the first use of Irrational Numbers, Quadratic Equations, of the form

$A.X^2 = C$ and $A.X^2 + B.X=C$

Pythagorean Theorem and Pythagorean triplets were found in Sulba Sutras

$A^2 = B^2 + C^2$

Many examples of Pythagorean triplets were given as the sides of right angled triangle.

JAIN Mathematics (400 B.C. - 400A.D.)

During this period, the theory of numbers was firmly established and classified into three sets: enumerable, innumerable and infinite.

Also found in their extensive work, were the key elements:

(a) Knowledge of the foundation laws of Indices.

(b) Arithmetic operations.

(c) Geometry

(d) Operations with fractions.

(e) Simple Equations.

(f) Cubic Equations.

(g) Quadratic Equations.

(h) Operations with Logarithms.

(i) Sequences and progressions

(j) Permutations and Combinations

The extensive work in permutation and combination resulted in to the formation of PASCAL TRIANGLE called MERU PRASTARA by the Jains. This was many centuries before Pascal invented the triangle and the theorem which states:

n+1 Cr = n Cr + n Cr-1

By permutation and combination,

n. C1 = n, n .C2= n (n-1)

n.C3 = n, n P2= n (n-1) = n (n-1) (n-

BAKSHALI MANUSCRIPT (2 B.C.—2 A.D.)

This was discovered in the 19 century. The historians claimed that this monumental work was the work of the Jain mathematicians. They are given very wide credit for ten principal discoveries:

1. Examples of the rules of three (profit /loss/interest)
2. Solutions of linear equations with as many as five unknowns

3. Quadratic equations
4. Arithmetic and geometric progressions
5. Compound Series
6. Quadratic indeterminate equations
7. Simultaneous equations
8. Fractions including the use of Zero
9. Negative sign
10. Improved method of calculating square root

One of the most important discoveries was the solution of a linear equation with five unknowns. An interesting example is given as:

Five merchants together want to buy a jewel. Its price is equal to half the money possessed by the first together with the money possessed by the others or one third the money possessed by the second together with the money of the others or ¼ money possessed by the third together with the money of the others. Find the price the jewel and money possessed by each merchant.

Solution: X½ + X2 + X 3 + X4 + X5 = P — Equation 1

X1 + X 2/3 + X3 + X 4 + X5 = P — Equation 2

X1 + X2 + X3/4 + X4 +X5 = P — Equation 3

X1 + X2 + X3 +X4/5 + X5 = P — Equation 4

X1 + X2 + X3 + X4 + X5/6 = P — Equation 5

Then if,

X1/2 + X2/3 +X3/4 + X4/5+ X5/6 = Q

The equation becomes (377/60) Q =P

A number of possible answers can be obtained. This is the origin of Indeterminate

Equation of the type A.X = Y. This theory was not only developed but perfected by Bhaskara2 about 400 years before its discovery in Europe.

The answer to the above question is:

If Q = 60, then P= 377

X1 = 120, X2 = 90, X3 = 80, X4 = 75 and X5= 72

The Bakhshali manuscript is a unique piece of work, while it not only contains mathematics of a remarkably high standard for the time period, also, in contrast to almost all other Indian works composed before and after, the method of commentary follows a highly systematic order of:

1. Statement of the rule.
2. statement of the examples
3. demonstration of the operations of the rule

By the end of the 2 century, mathematics in India had attained a considerable stature and had become divorced from purely practical and religious requirements.

Although, it is worth noting that over the next 1000 years, the majority of mathematical developments occurred within the works of astronomy.

The topics of algebra, arithmetic and geometry had developed significantly and it is widely thought that the Decimal place value had been perfected by year 200A.D. The consequences of that work were wide spread.

The Decimal Numeration (Ref. 1, 2 &5)

This system was developed in India in about 1000B.C. But the credit was erroneously given to Babylonians and Greeks without any foundation. During the excavation of Harrapa in the Indus Valley, they discovered symbols with a system that uses the numbers from 1 through 9. The inventor of Zero is unknown. Zero was denoted by a dot, then by a circle with a dot in the center and later by an oval shape we use now. An extensive description of the decimal system has been noted by on buildings, sculptures and altars. The French mathematician, Laplace describes the invention of the decimal system as: "The idea of expressing all quantities by nine numbers whereby is imparted to them both an absolute value and one by position is so simple that this very simplicity is the very reason for our not being sufficiently aware how much admiration it deserves" (Ref. 5).

Having become firmly established in academic circles in India by the 6th century the decimal system value spread across the world, initially, to China and Egypt and then to the Arab world. Arabic scholars during this time improved the system by introducing decimal fractions. The system also spread into Spain and by 16 the century, was accepted in Europe.

The invention of zero had a monumental impact on the entire mathematical system. In the words of G. Halstead, the famous mathematician (Ref. 4) who commented: The importance of the creation of the Zero mark can never be exaggerated. This giving to airy nothing, not merely a local habituation and a name, a picture, a symbol but helpful power, is the characteristic of the Hindu Race whence it sprang. No single mathematical creation has been more potent for the general on go of intelligence and power.

The Classical Period 1500 B.C.-700 A.D.

The establishment of the Gupta dynasty, a period of political stability across India, contributed to the ascent of a galaxy of mathematicians and astronomers led by Aryabhata. A native of Kerala, he covered the following subjects:

(a) Method of inversion
(b) Various arithmetic operations such as cubes, cube root, squares and square roots
(c) Formulae and rules for finding the sum of several types of series.
(d) Rule of three
(e) Rules for solving examples on interest which led to quadratic equation
(f) Tables of sines
(g) Area of triangles
(h) Volume rules.

The Aryabhata work was translated into Arabic by Abdul Al Hasson-Alwazi (1000B.C.) (Ref. 1&4). Diophantus, the father of Greek algebra got the first algebraic knowledge from India. (Ref. R.C.Gupta, Journal of Mathematics Education, 10, B60-73, 1976). Numerous examples of algebraic equations are given in the reference which led to the establishment of the Pythagorean Theorem.

Aryabhata's work on astronomy was also pioneering and was far less tinged with a mythological flavor. Among many theories, he was the first one to suggest that diurnal motion of the "heavens" is due to the rotation of the earth about its axis, which is incredibly important (Ref. 4). In the field of pure mathematics, his most significant contribution was his solution to the indeterminate equation:

$$ax - by = c$$

Although Indian mathematics has become often ignored, this was not always the case. The Aryabhatiya was translated into Arabic by 1000A.D.as Zij-al-Arjabhar (Ref.4). It is partly through this translation that Indian computational and mathematical methods were introduced to the Arabs which led to the forward progress made by mathematics.

Bhaskara (600 A.D. – 680 A.D).

He was a prominent astronomer and his work in that area gave rise to an extremely accurate approximation for the Sine Function. His commentary in the mathematical sections, and he developed several of the ideas contained within. Perhaps, his most important contribution was that which he made to the topic of Algebra.

After Aryabhata's death around 550A.D, the work of BRAHMAGUPTA resulted in Indian mathematics attaining an even greater level of perfection.

Brahmagupta 598 A.d. - 665 A.d

He was the most prominent mathematician of the so-called Ujjain School of Mathematics.

1. He was the first one to divide by zero which led to $n/0 = \infty$ (infinity) and demonstrated the advanced understanding of an extremely abstract concept.

2. Theory of arithmetic progression
3. Algorithm for calculating square roots that is equivalent to the Newton-Raphson iterative formula, but clearly predates Newton by many centuries.

Geometry

1. Established rules for calculating diagonals of cyclic quadrilaterals
2. Right angled triangles

Algebra

1. Solved a number of equations such as $ax + c = by$
2. Established two solutions for quadratic equations
3. Calculated an interpolation formula used to calculate
4. values of Sines bears resemblance to the Newton-Sterling interpolation formula

Gupta (Ref.3) mentions that the spread of Buddhism (500 A.D.) into China resulted in a period of cultural activities and Brahmagupta's work spread rapidly.

Bhaskaracharya 2 Or Bhaskara 2

Bhaskara2 is regarded as perhaps the greatest Hindu mathematician of all time and his contribution to not just Indian but world mathematics is undeniable. Born in 1114A.D. in Bijapur, India, he became the head of the Ujjain School of mathematical astronomy (Ref. 1, 2, 4 & 5). He wrote Siddhanta Siromani (SS) in 1150A.D. which contains four sections:

(a) Lilawati (Arithmatic)
(b) Bijaganita (Algebra)
(c) Goladhyaya (sphere/celestial globe)
(d) Grahaganita (Mathematics of planets)

Mr. Joseph (Ref. 5) states that Bhaskara's significant works were Lilawati, Bijaganita and his work on astronomy.

Lilawati (or Leelavati) is divided into 13 chapters and covers every branch of mathematics, arithmetic and geometry. More specifically, the contents include:

(a) Definitions
(b) Property of Zero (including division)
(c) Further extensive numerical work, including the use of negative numbers
(d) Estimation of (pi)
(e) Arithmetical terms, methods of multiplication, squaring, inverse rule of three, plus rules of 5, 7 and 9
(f) Problems involving interest
(g) Arithmetic and geometric progressions
(h) Plane geometry.
(i) Solid geometry.
(j) Combinations.
(k) Indeterminate equations (kuttaka), integer solutions (first and second order)

His contributions to the last topic were important which led to further work on the shadow of Gnomon.

Bijaganita is effectively a treatise on Algebra and contains the following subjects:

(a) Positive and negative numbers.
(b) Zero
(c) Simple equations(indeterminate of second, third and fourth degree)
(d) Simple equations with more than one unknown
(e) Quadratic equations with more than one unknown
(f) Operations with products of several unknowns

Bhaskara derived a cyclic, 'Cakraval' method for solving equations of the form $ax^2 + bx + c = y$ which is usually attributed to William Brouncker who rediscovered it around 1657. Bhaskara's method for finding the solutions of the problem $N.x^2 + 1 = y^2$ (so called Pell's Equation) is of considerable interest and importance.

Bhaskara is thought to be the first to show that:

$$\delta \sin x = \cos x .\delta x$$

Evidence suggests that Bhaskara was fully acquainted with the principle of differential calculus and he further showed that the differential coefficient vanishes as an extreme value of the function, indicating knowledge of the concept of "Infinitesimals".

He also gave results for sin (a + b) and sin (a-b). This is an early form of Rolle's theorem.

Pell's Equation

Although there were great advancements in many areas of Algebra and solution of simple form such as ax + c=y to forms as complex as $ax^2 + bxy + cy^2 = z^2$, let us^{2}a mistake by Euler whoattributed the equation to John Pell, a 17 century Englishmathematician. The equation wasnearly solved by Brahmagupta (628 A.D.) and further improved by Bhaskara. The complete theoryunderlying the solution was expounded by French mathematician, LaGrange in 1767 and rests on the theory of continued fractions. Brahmagupta's remarkable achievement involves an element of trail process but contains no mention of continued fractions. Instead, itused square roots extensively. The similar method was used by Newton and Raphson in 1690which is now known as Newton-Raphson Iterative Method.The Pell's type of equation was known in India as Varga Prakriti or equation of Multiplied Square where Prakriti means Coefficient and refers to the coefficient N (where N is a positive integer). As mentioned earlier, Bhaskara developed a Chakravala or cyclic method of solution.

The following example is of great interest and is found in Bijaganita. The same example was used by the French mathematician, Fermat in 1657. Solution of $67 x^2 +1 = y^2$

The auxiliary equation 67 x 12 – 3 = 82 can be used.

Then using Bhaskara's method where $Na^2 +k = b^2$ where a, b and k are the integers (1, -3 and 8) in the auxiliary equation above, (k being positive or negative), then,

$$N (am + b) / k^2 + ((m^2\text{-}N)/ k) = ((b m + N a)/K)^2$$

Thus,

67 ((1.m + 8)/-3)^2 + ((m2—67)/—3)) = (8 m +67x1)/-3)^2 Equation 1

By the method of Kuttaka, the solution of (m+8)/-3 = an integer, is m = –3 t + 1

Putting t= –2, we get m=7 which makes (m^2- 67) least

On substituting this value, Equation 1 reduces to:

$$67 \times 52 + 6 = 412$$

Bhaskara then proceeded and used the principle of composition of equals and more use of Kuttaka; he came to the final solution as:

X = 5967 and Y= 48842 is a solution of the equation: 67.x^2 + 1 = y^2

In the above mentioned work by Bhaskara, I have taken the liberty of quoting from References 2, 3, 4 and 5. The use of square roots of the integer and the cyclic method were widely used for the first time. Similar techniques were used much later in Europe by famous mathematicians such as Fermat, La Grange, Bernoulli and Leibniz.

PART 2: The End of the Classical Period:1400 A.D.-1600 A.D.

The works by Bhaskara 2 was considered the highest point Indian mathematics attained and it was long considered that Indian mathematics ceased after that point.

Shortly after Bhaskara's death, India was engulfed in war (Mongol Invasion) and political turmoil. Consequently, the atmosphere of security and tranquility was lost which was doubtlessly a major contributory factor to the barrenness of scientific activity and achievement. As C. Srinivasan (Ref. 4) quotes: India suddenly fell apart into a state of "Torpor" and never recovered from this torpor until the advent of mathematicians trained according to Western methods.

There were occasional small developments and attempts to improve the knowledge of mathematics but nothing of the magnitude of the previous millennium.

Recent discoveries have found that despite political turmoil, mathematics did continue to a high degree in South India up to the

16 century. The Southern part of India avoided the worst of the political upheavals of the sub-continent and the so called Kerala School flourished for some time producing some truly remarkable results.

It is worth mentioning that just after Bhaskara's death the knowledge of the Indian mathematics had exerted a great influence on Arabic works. Although

Arabic scholars relied on a variety of sources including the Babylonians, Syria, Greek, and some Chinese texts, Indian mathematical texts played a major role. Scholars such as Ibn Tariq and Al Fazari (8 century, Baghdad) Al-Kindi (9 century, Basra) and Al-khwarizmi (9 century Khiva) were amongst the many that based their works on Indian texts.

Part 3: Keralese Mathematics: 1400-1800 A.D.

The south western tip of India escaped the majority of the political upheaval which engulfed the rest of the country and allowed a generally peaceful existence to continue. Thus, the pursuit of advancement of mathematics continued uninterrupted for a couple of centuries. It has recently been discovered that Kerala mathematics was strongly influence by Astronomy and this led to the derivation of mathematical results of huge importance. More research is going on and that will shed more light on Kerala mathematics. There is also interest in the claims that European scholars may have had first hand knowledge of Kerala mathematics.

Narayan Pandit (1340-1400A.D.), the earliest of the Kerala scholars had written two works, an arithmetical treatise called Ganita Kaumudi and algebraic treatise called Bijaganita Vatamsa. He was strongly influenced by Bhaskara 2.Pandit's work was written in conjunction with another scholar, Sankara Variyar.

Narayan's other major works include a variety of mathematical developments including a rule to calculate approximate values of square roots, using the second order indeterminate equation $N x^2 +1 = y^2$ (Pell's equation). R.Gupta (Ref. 2) has also brought to light Narayan's contribution to the topic of cyclic quadrilaterals.

Paramesvera (1370-1460A.D.), Narayan Pandit's student developed the Mean value theorem and a mean value type formula for inverse interpolation of Sine and is believed to be the first mathematician to give the Radius of Circle with inscribed cyclic quadrilateral, an expression that is normally attributed to Lhuilier (1782).

Nilkantha Somayajii (1444-1544A.D.) was a disciple of Paramesvara. He apparently contributed to two volumes but unfortunately, his books are lost. But his prominent work was:

$$\tan^{-1} t = t - t^3/3 + -$$

widely mentioned in Madhava's wok.

Madhava (15century) in Kochi together with Nilkantha contributed to the classical modern analysis particularly in advanced geometry which was a forerunner to their work on astronomy.

Possible Transmission Of Keralese Mathematics To Europe

A recent article by D.Almeida, J.John and A. Zordozhnyy (Journal of Natural Geometry, 20, 77-104, 2001) suggests that the knowledge of Kerala was transmitted to Europe from 16 century onwards. There were few sources for such a transmission. Kerala had a very well educated Jesuit missionary presence for over 1000 years. Further, there was a well-established and well educated Jews in Kerala for many years. Both these groups traveledextensively by ships from Kerala to the Middle East and later to Europe. This is being researched and more evidence is being assembled. However, the current theory is that the Kerala calculus and mathematics remained localized until its discovery by Charles Whish in the late 19th century.

Conclusion

I am not a mathematician by profession but have studied mathematics as an undergraduate and a graduate student and I love the subject. From my limited research, I have been able to compile the history of ancient Indian mathematics. This I did with the help from many scholars mentioned in my references. I am sure I have made some mistakes and please do not hesitate to point out so I can make the necessary corrections.

I have come to the conclusion that the work of Indian mathematicians from about 4000 B.C. to about 1600 A.D. had been severely neglected or purposely distorted. What could be the motivations behind this may have many reasons. First is the establishment of the principal of European domination from Archimedes to Pythagoras, Newton, Leibniz was essential in the later phase of colonial dominance over Asia and the Middle East. This was the way to show the European superiority in every sphere of life including mathematics. The second reason may be the religious differences between Europe and Asia. Some of the ideas from the East such as India were not well received and thereby neglected. As more research is being conducted in this history of mathematics, more facts will beknown todraw better conclusions.

References

1. Dwary, N.N. - Mathematics in ancient and medieval India, Journal of mathematical Education, 8, 39-44. 1991.
2. Gupta, R.C. - Highlights of mathematical developments in India, Journal of Mathematical Education, 20, 138, 1986.
3. Gupta, R.C. - Development of Algebra *Journal of mathematical Education, 10, 1 53-6, 1976.*
4. Boyer, C.B. - A history of mathematics, John Wiley and Sons, 1968.
5. Joseph, G.G. - The crest of the peacock, non-European roots of mathematics Princeton University Press, 2000.

Chapter - 2

What are the reasons for excellence in mathematics?

In Ancient India

Many researchers in the history of Indian mathematics have asked this question and to the best of my knowledge have not been able to answer satisfactorily.

"Why is it so hard to find information about Indian mathematics"? There are three groups of researchers who have attempted to solve this problem: Group one consists of non-Indologists who attempt to integrate the Indian tradition into the history of mathematical sciences elsewhere in the world. Group two are Indians who are predominantly Hindu mathematicians and they do not question anything beyond what they read. Their objectivity in my opinion is not satisfactory. Group three are mathematicians devoted to understand the precise reasons but because of scarcity of reliable date and some unique challenges in translation have not advanced beyond some vague rationale. (Ref. 1, 2)

I do not have answers to the question either but in this article, I am showing different factors which come into play in the ancient Indian mathematical history and try to point out the interactions so that I will let the reader decide the reasons for excellence in mathematics in ancient India.

Factor 1: World History Timeline (The following is for the India only) (Ref. 3)

A: 9000-5000 B.C.

1. 7500B.C. Ancient bricks at the Gulf of Cambay in the state of Punjab in India. Remains of what may have been a pre-Hardpan city.
2. 7000 B.C. – Earliest pre- Harrapan settlement of Mehragath.
3.

B: 4000-3000 B.C

4. Excavations from this period at Summerian sites of Kish and Susa Reveal existence of Indian trade products. (Summeria air a part of Syria-Iraq)
5. 3000B.C. Egyptian Hieroglyphs developed
6.

C: 3000-2500 B.C.

7. 2600-1800 B.C. – Indus civilization at its height. The Harrapan cities have Sophisticated water and sewer systems, the likes of which would not be Seen until Roman times in England.
8. 2586 B.C. – The temple of Sri-Rangam in south India completed.

   (The first Egyptian pyramid was built in 2700 B.C.)

D: 1600- 1500 B.C.

9. 1500 B.C. –Cinnamon is exported from Kerala to Middle East.

E: 300 B.C. –10 A.D.

10. 150 B.C. – Ajanta Buddhists caves have started near Hyderabad, India
11. 50 B.C. – Kushana Empire begins in India. This Mongolian Buddhists dynasty rules most of India, Afghanistan and parts of Central Asia

F: 10 A.D.

12. Indian embassy was established in Rome –Emperor Trajan

13.

Factor 2: The Sanskrit Language: The language plays a key role in the Development of Indian Mathematics (Ref. 4)

Discover Sanskrit

Where did it begin: Sanskrit (SAMSKRTA meaning 'perfected, refined or polished) is the ancient sacred language of India and is believed to be the oldest in the world? The origin of Sanskrit can be accredited to the VEDIC society. Vedic Sanskrit is believed to date back to 4000 B.C. when knowledge was handed down through generations verbally. Mystic traditions of India ascribe a wholly sacred origin to the language describing it as the language of the gods. It was Sir William Jones who took serious interest in Sanskrit and he said Sanskrit possessed vocabulary and structure very similar to Greek, Latin and even English.

According to literature, by year 4000 B.C., a Hindu Grammarian by the name of Panini had formally recorded rules of Sanskrit grammar. (Incidentally, the latest story is Panini was born in Afghanistan). Panini's grammar is called Ashtadhyayi. It consists of 8 chapters, each divided into four sections of "Padas". It characterizes the difference between the language of the sacred texts and that of the common street language. 3959 rules of Sanskrit morphology have been set out, ***Much In The Way of Mathematical Function,*** to define the basic elements of the language including the sentence structure., vowels, consonants, nouns, and verbs. Panini's work is still used to day in teaching of Sanskrit.

Classical Sanskrit, as compared to more archaic ancestor, Vedic Sanskrit was at its height in the centuries A.D. From it came a vast body of philosophical, scientific, and religious knowledge as well as Hindu scriptures And classical literature.

Factor 3: The framework of Indian History, Geography and Formative Period.

Important reasons for India's distinctive path lie in the geography and early historical experiences. India's topography shaped a number of vital features of its civilization. The vast Indian sub-continent is partially separated

From the rest of Asia (and particularly from East Asia) by northern mountain Ranges. Mountain passes linked India to civilizations in the Middle East. Though it was not as isolated as China, the sub-continent was set apart within Asia. (In my opinion, these mountain passes happen to be a small advantage to India but a big curse because that was the way invaders came and destroyed one of the finest civilizations the world has seen). The most important agricultural reasons are along the two rivers, the Ganges and the Indus.

By 600B.C. India had passed through its formative stage. Indian development did not take on the structure of rising and falling dynasties as in China.

Factor 4: Vedic Mathematics:

The Sanskrit word Vedic means knowledge and the Vedas are considered to be the most sacred scriptures of Hinduism referred to as Sutras, meaning what was revealed to the seers. Vedas are considered the most ancient scriptures dealing with all branches of knowledge – spiritual and worldly.

Some chronological confusion exists with regards to the appearance of Vedic religion. S.Kak (Ref. 4) states in recent work that the time period for the Vedic religion stretches back potentially as far as 8000 B.C. and definitely 4000 B.C. Where as G. Joseph (Ref. 1) states 1500 B.C. as the forming of the Hindu civilization and the recording of the Vedas and Vedangas and later Sulbasutras. However, it seems most likely that significant knowledge of astronomy and mathematics first appears in Vedic works around 2000 B.C.

The RIG VEDA (fire altar) the earliest extent Vedic works dates from 1900 B.C. R.Gupta (Ref. 6) in his paper on the problem of Indian chronology shows that dates from 2600 to 200 B.C. have been suggested as the Vedic period. After reading many sources, I have come to the conclusion that the period of Vedas is 1900—1000 B.C.

It is worth mentioning that although the requirements of mathematics at that time was clearly not for its own sake, but for the purpose of religion and astronomy, it is important not to IGNORE the secular use of the texts, i.e.,

By the craftsmen who were building the altars.

(I must confess I do not understand the tremendous forward step from religious rites to very essence of fundamental mathematics. Where does this knowledge come from? I have not seen any reference to understand the very analytical steps required for the background and the process of bringing in mathematics. Either mathematics or arithmetic was already there and was being developed separately and some geniuses put the entire package together to make look that Mathematics and Vedas grew together. Much more research is necessary to convince the readers.)

S.Kak (Ref. 4), an authority on the astronomical content of the Vedic works shows surprising evidences for various astronomical quantities such as the relative sizes of the planets, the distance of the earth from the sun, the length of the day, and the length of the year. Much of the mathematics contained within the Vedas is found in works called Vedangas of which there are six.

Of the six Vedangas, those of particular interest are Vedangas Jyotis and Kalpa (the fifth and the sixth Vedangas). Jyoti was the name for astronomy and Kalpa was the name for Hindu rituals and ceremonies. N.Dwary (Ref. 7) claims, with reference to the Vedangas –Jyoti, that:

"Hindus of the period were fully conversant with fundamental operations Of Arithmetic".

Along with the Vedanta's, there are several further works that contain mathematics including:

Tattiriya Samhita
Satpatha Brahmana
Yajur-Atharva Veda
Rg-veda
Samhitas

These books include a fundamental description of mathematics:

- Use of Geometry

- Equivalence through numbers and area,
- Equivalence led to the problem of squaring the circle
- Early form of Pythagorean Theorem,
- Estimation of ð
- All four arithmetic operators (addition, subtraction, division and Multiplication
- A definite system of for denoting any number up to 1055
- Existence of Zero
- Prime numbers

Evidence of the use of this advanced numerical concept leads S. Sinha to conclude:

"It is fair to agree that a nation with such an advanced and cultural civilization and which was using the numerical system (decimal place values) knew also how to handle the associated arithmetic." (Ref. 8).

Factor 5: Some nuggets from Vedic Mathematics:

As described earlier, Vedas are ancient holy texts from India than can be legitimately characterized as all- encompassing repository of Hindu Knowledge from years past. R.Gupta (Ref. 6) has shown some excellent examples of how Vedic knowledge in the form of Shlokas or poems in Sanskrit verse are encoded in numbers. This system uses consonant groups of the Sanskrit alphabet and vowels and the numbers. The coding is given as KAADI NAV, TAADI NAV. PADI PANCHAK, and YAADASHTAK TA KSHA SHUNYAM. This is translated below:

- Letter "KA" and the following 8 letters.
- Letter "TA" and the following 8 letters.
- Letter "PA" and the following 4 letters.
- Letter "YA" and following 7 letters.
- Letter "KSHA" for ZERO

In other words,

Ka, ta, pa, ya, = 1

Kha, tha, pha, ra = 2

Ga, da, ba, la =3 Gha, dha, bha, scha, = 4

Gna, na, ma, scha = 5
Cha, ta, sha = 6
Chha, tha, sa = 7
Ja, da, ha = 8
Jha, dha = 9
Kasha = 0

I am trying to simplify in the following way:

Ka, kah, gha, gna
Cha, chha, ja, jha, jnya
Ta, tha dad ha na
Pa pha ba bha ma
Ya ra la vas cha
Sha sa ha chjha tra gna

Thus, PA PA is 11, MA RA is 52. Words KAPA, TAPA, PAPA, YAPA mean the same, that is 11

The author had to choose one system that fit the meaning of the verse well. An interesting example is a hymn below in the praise of God Krishna that gives the value of PIE (π) to the 32 decimal places as

O.31415026535897328446243338327920

Gopi bhaagya madhu Vraata
Shringisho dadhisandhiga
Khalajivita khaatsaava
Galahaataarasandhara

This analogy and example is absolutely fantastic beyond description.

Let me continue briefly the method that was used to calculate.

1. EKADHIKENA PURVENA (or By one more than the previous one) The proposition "By" means the operation this Sutra concerns are either multiplication or division. (In the case of addition/subtraction proposition 'to' or 'from' is used). Thus, this Sutra is used for either multiplication, or division. It turns out that it is applicable in both operations.

An interesting application for this Sutra is in computing Squares, of numbers ending in five. Consider:

$$35 \times 35 = (3\ (3+1))\ 25 = 12,\ 25$$

The latter portion is multiplied by itself (5 × 5) and the previous portion is multiplied by more than itself (3 by 4) resulting in the answer 1225.

It can also be used in multiplication, division and subtraction.

I am purposely avoiding going into details because I try not to test your patience.

Factor 6: Mathematics and the Language of Nature

This is my philosophical approach because I think it fits well in this environment .

"God is a mathematician", so said Sir James Jeans (Ref. 9). In a series of books and articles published in the 1930's, the British astronomer suggested that the Universe arises out of pure thought that is couched in the language of Abstract Mathematics. But why should God think only in mathematics? After all, some of the most impressive achievements of the human race have involved architecture, poetry, drama and art. Could the essence of mathematics not equally be captured in a prose or a poem ?

While there are exceptions, it is generally true that great mathematics is studied for its own sake and without reference to anything outside itself.

Mathematics has a beauty of its own and there is, for the mathematician, an aesthetic joy that comes from solving an important problem, no matter what value society may place on this activity. In this sense, mathematics has constantly sought to free itself from its practical origins.

Geometry, for example, began with rules for surveying, calculating the areas of fields and making astronomical studies acts of navigation. The English mathematician, Professor G. Hardy (Srinivas Ramanujan's tutor at Cambridge University, U.K.) refused to justify mathematics in terms of its utility and pursued as an art for its sake. Indeed,

Hardy once spoke of a monument so high that no one would ever be able to see the statue that was placed at its pinnacle – a fitting metaphor for its own, somewhat extreme, view of the role of mathematics. (Ref. 10)

It is common to talk and write of "the language of mathematics". But is mathematics really a language? Clearly, mathematics does not have the same fluency as a natural language and even more obviously, it is rarely spoken aloud. This, to me, suggests mathematics is really a more restrictive form of language. Nevertheless, the suggestion is that everything mathematics can do must ultimately find its origin in language.

I tend to think that this rationale of relationship between language (Sanskrit) written in forms of Vedas and mathematics developed may be one of the reasons to our main question.

Conclusion

In this article, I have provided six factors which may explain the reasons why mathematics prospered in ancient India 2000 B.C. while the rest of the world was living in uncivilized manner. Unfortunately, there must be some other factors involved which have not been covered. The early Indians were not super humans to create a totally revolutionary concept of mathematics that we know today. Who were these people? What caused them to think in some abstract way? How did they think to combine the language and transfer the knowledge to mathematics. I have not seen any answer to these fundamental questions. Hope future research will provide some definite answers.

I would like your cooperation after you read this article. Please let me know if you have some ideas to my questions and I will pursue them because I am very much interested in knowing the truth.

References

1. Joseph, G. G. (2000) The Crest of the Peacock, non-European roots of Mathematics, PrincetonUniversity Press
2. History of Mathematics (2002) at St. Andrews University, Scotland, U.K.
3. Archaeology on line (1999).

4. Kak, S.C. (1993) Astronomy of the Vedic altars, Vistas in astronomy 36, 117-140.
5. Classical Civilization in India : wps. Ablongman/long- Sterns (1989).
6. Gupta, R.C. (1986), Highlights of mathematical development in India. The Mathematics Education (Historical), 8, 131- 138.
7. Dwary, N.N. (1991), Mathematics in ancient and medieval India. The Mathematics education (historical), 8, 39-41.
8. Sinha, R.S.(1981), Contributions of ancient Indian mathematicians. The Mathematics Education, 15, 659-82.
9. Sir James Jeans (1930), The Mysterious Universe – Cambridge University Press.
10. Professor G. Hardy – CambridgeUniversity Press (1967).

Chapter - 3

The Role of Mathematics in the Development of Sanskrit

The world famous nuclear scientist and Nobel Laureate, Niels Bohr was constantly emphasizing the role played by the language in science and mathematics so that people can investigate the key concepts for discussion. My objective in this article is to show the roles of Sanskrit (mother of Indo –European languages) and mathematics played to create the excellence in both the subjects and the best in the ancient Indian civilization (4000 B.C. – 1400 A.D.)

I will begin with the definitions of a Language and Mathematics and their interdependence and relate successes of both to the progress of a civilization.

What is a language?

1. A systematic means of communication by the use of sounds or conventional symbols.
2. A system of words used in a particular discipline
3. The code we all use to express ourselves and communicate with others.
4. A set (finite and infinite) of sentences, each finite in length and constructed out of finite set of elements.

   These definitions describe a language in terms of the following components:

   (a) A vocabulary of symbols and words

(b) A grammar consisting of rules of how these symbols may be used

(c) A community of people who use and understand these symbols

(d) A range of meanings that can be communicated with these symbols

What is mathematics?

Mathematics is used to communicate information about a wide range of different subjects. Here are the broad categories:

A. Mathematics describes the real world: Many areas of mathematics originated with attempts to describe and solve real world problems and solve real world phenomena – from measuring farms (geometry) to falling apples (calculus) to gambling (probability). Mathematics has also been widely used in modern physics and engineering, and has helped us to understand the universe around us.

B. Mathematics describes abstract structures. : Pure Mathematics also describes entities which have no physical counterparts at all. However, it is difficult to give any categorical examples here, as even the most abstract structures can be co-opted as models. (String theory for example)

C. Mathematics describes Metamathematics: It can be used reflexively to describe itself—this is an area of mathematics called Metamathematics.

Both these definitions were summarized by a well-known German mathematician, R.E. Schwarzenegger (2000) as: My own attitude, which I share with many of my colleagues, is simply that Mathematics is a Language, like English or Latin or Sanskrit. There are certain concepts for which mathematics is particularly well suited: It would be foolish to write a love poem in the language of mathematics to prove the Fundamental Theorem of Algebra.

Mathematics as a language

It is common to talk of "the language of mathematics". But is mathematics a language? Does it possess various properties that are characteristic of other natural languages? Clearly, mathematics does not have the same fluency as a natural language and even, more obviously, it is rarely spoken aloud. This really suggests that Mathematics is really a more Restrictive Limited form of language. But it is very important to bear that everything mathematics can do must ultimately find its origin in a language.

In all the following pages, the dates are tentative because recent research has shown some revised dates which I have used in this article. The proof is not totally established.

The two subjects, Language in this case, Sanskrit and Indian mathematics are initially dealt separately. I will then try to show these two subjects are inter-dependent and both flourished to create the excellence which lasted for a few centuries.

Discover Sanskrit

Where did it begin?

Sanskrit (Samskrta: meaning Perfect, Refined or Polished) is the ancient language of India. An official language of India is believed to be the oldest language of the world. There are still hundreds of millions of people who use Sanskrit in their daily lives, but despite these numbers, its cultural worth is unsurpassed. The origin of Sanskrit is accredited to the Vedic Society (Ref. 1). Vedic Sanskrit is believed to date back to 2000 B.C. when knowledge was handed down verbally through generations.

How did it begin?

By 500 B.C. approximately, a Hindu grammarian by the name of Panini had formally recorded the rules of Sanskrit grammar (Ref. 2). This is known as the Ashtadhyayi. It consists of eight chapters, each divided into four sections or "Padas". It characterizes the difference between the Language of the Sacred and that of the Common People. 3959 rules of Sanskrit morphology have been set out, much in the way of Mathematical Function, to define the basic elements of the language including the sentence structure, vowels, consonants, nouns and verbs. Panini's work is still used today in the teaching of Sanskrit. Classical Sanskrit as opposed to its more archaic ancestor Vedic Sanskrit was used earlier in writing of mathematics.

Mystic traditions of India ascribe a wholly sacred origin to the language of Gods. When Westerners began to take interest in the Sanskrit language two hundred years ago, Sir William Jones (Ref. 3), introduced to Europe the antiquity and true merits of Indian literature, language and culture. He originally went to India to work as a Supreme Court judge in Calcutta. Proficient in many European languages from an early age, he developed an interest in the study of Indian culture and civilization. Among the many projects he undertook, worth mentioning, were his translation of the works of Kalidasa (a well-known Indian writer). Sir William Jones was the first to suggest that Sanskrit originated from the same source as Latin, Greek and Persian, thus laying the foundation for the comparative study of what we now refer to as Indo-European languages. In a lecture in 1786, Sir William made the following statement which aroused the curiosity of many scholars. He declared: Sanskrit language whatever be its antiquity, is of wonderful structure; more perfect then Greek, more copious then the Latin and more exquisitely refined then either, yet bearing to both of them a stronger affinity, both in the roots of verbs and in the forms of grammar, then could not possibly have been produced by accident; so strong indeed, that no philosopher could examine them all three, without believing them to have sprung from some common source, which perhaps no longer exists. (Jones Collected Works, Vol. 3, 34-35 ed. Lord Teignmouth 13 vols. London, John Stockdale.).

The Proto-Indo-European Language – PIE

The statement of Sir William Jones was both revelatory and revolutionary. It shook the foundations of the age old European belief that Hebrew was the source of languages. This work led to comparative study of the origin and evolution of Indo-European languages or simply PIE. The following languages are supposed to have been derived from Sanskrit and are classified as:

1. Indo-Iranian divided into Indic (Indo-Aryan) composing of Sanskrit and its derivative languages and Iranian languages, most popular amongst them being Dagestan, Persian and Pashto.
2. Baltic: Lithuanian, Latvian etc.
3. Slavic: Russian, Polish, Serbia-Croatia etc.

4. Armenian: Albania
5. Greek
6. Celtic: Irish, Scottish, Welsh
7. Romance: Italian, French, Spanish, Portuguese, Romanian,
8. Germanic: German, English, Dutch, and Scandinavian languages
9. Italic: Latin
10. Anatolian: Hittite, Palaic.
11. Tocharian: also called Tocarish was spoken in Northern China and used by early Buddhists.
12.

There are many reasons why I went into detail in these origin of languages is simply because the foundation and the structure laid in all the languages was a prelude to the advancement of mathematics which is also highly structured.

Discover Mathematics

In the early civilizations, the first expression of mathematical understanding appears in the form of counting systems using sticks. Numbers in very early societies were typically represented by groups of lines, though later different numbers came to be assigned specific numeral names and symbols. This was in India and the time period roughly was 3000—2000B.C. (Ref. 4). After this initial period, mathematics was developed along with the development of Sanskrit. The sacred Vedas, whose names literally mean "knowledge", are often considered the formation of learning. The genre of "Vedic texts" embraces the four Samhistas or collection of hymns and rituals –namely, the Rig-Veda, Yajur-Veda, Sama-Veda, and Atharva-Veda. All these Vedas set the stage for performing religious sacrifices and this knowledge was shaped in around 1000B.C. What do these texts tell us about ancient Indian ideas on mathematical subjects? In the first place, they reveal that early Vedic times, a regularized Decimal system of number words to express quantity was well established. (Most of these numbers evidently date back as far as PIE since they have many similarities in other Indo-European languages.

Some simple fractional parts such as one third, using ordinal number forms as in their English equivalents also occur in Early or Middle Vedic texts. (For example in Yajur-Veda, "He, Vishnu, set himself in three places, a third on the Earth, a third in the atmosphere, a third in the sky."

No later than the Middle Vedic period, the Indian decimal integers had been expanded to a remarkable extent with the addition of number words for much larger powers of ten, up to at least a trillion (10^{12}). The first record of them occurs among the hymns included in the Yajur-Veda's description of sacrificial rites. These hymns invoke not only deities but also some aspects of nature and abstract entities, including various sequences of numbers, both round and compound (Ref. 5).

Why did Vedic culture construct such an extensive number system and acclaim it in sacred texts? The computing requirements of everyday life would not have demanded more than a few decimal orders of magnitude, as seen among other ancient civilizations, whose number words reach only into thousands and tens of thousands. Although infinite speculations are possible about meta-physical or spiritual implications of these numbers in Vedic thoughts, I have not come across any conclusive evidence in this mystery.

The cosmic significance of numbers and arithmetic in rituals reflecting concepts of the universe is brought out clearly in another early 1000B.C. text, the Sata-Patha-Brahmana or the Brahamana of a thousand paths, an additional text describing the symbolism of the sacrificial rituals. The following passage refers to sacrificial fire altars made of baked bricks which symbolize the 720 days and nights of an ideal year. The creator God, Prajapati, representing this year and the concept of time in general, sought to regain power over his creation by arranging these 720 bricks in various ways: Prajapati, the year has created all existing things - Having created all existing things, he felt like one emptied out, and was afraid of death. He bethought himself "How can I get these beings back into my body?" and he divided his body into two: there were 360 bricks in the one and as many in the other; He did not succeed. He made himself six bodies of hundred and twenty bricks each. He did not succeed. He did not divide seven fold. He made himself eight bodies of ninety bricks each. He did not divide eleven fold. He did not either thirteen fold or twenty fold and did not succeed then, he stopped, at the fifteenth and because he stopped at the fifteenth arrangement, there is fifteen hours of the waxing and fifteen hours of waning (moon). And because he made himself twenty-four bodies, therefore, the year consists of twenty-four half months. (This example is from Prof. Poker's book, Page 15). The final division of 720 into 24 × 30 is the last possible one that will give an integer quotient. Even more interesting, mathematically speaking, than Prajapati's ultimate successful division are the divisions that he did not attempt, which would have produced fractional numbers of the bricks. The Concept of Integer Divisibility is thus a part of this cosmic narrative. Later, Vedic texts such as the Upanisads as well as contemporary Buddhists and Jain philosophy also offer intriguing possibilities of speculation about the development of some concepts later incorporated in mathematics per se. Examples of these include the synonymous Sunya and Kha, meaning void and nullify (In later mathematical terms Zero) and the Purena or fullness. It is now an established fact that all the Vedic texts clearly indicate long-standing tradition of decimal numeration and a deep fascination with various concepts of finite and infinite quantities and their significance in the Cosmos (Ref. 6).

Mathematical ideas were also explored in more concrete detail in some of the ancillary works classified as VEDANGAS, limb of the Vedas. These were in the form of phonetics, grammar, metrics, and astronomy ritual practices. Some of the ritual practice texts explain how the different types or goals of sacrifices were associated with different sizes and shapes of the Fire Altars, which were constructed from the baked bricks of prescribed numbers and dimensions. The foot - prints for the Altars were laid out on a leveled ground by manipulating chords of various lengths attached to stakes. The manuals described the required manipulation in terse, cryptic phrases——usually prose, sometimes verses called Sutras (literally "string" or rules, instructions). The measuring chord called Sulba gave the name to this set as Sulba-sutra or the Rules of the Cord.

Note: Popular usage of the term "Vedic Mathematics" often differs considerably from the mathematical content actually attested in Vedic texts. Some authors use Vedic Mathematics to mean the entire Sanskrit mathematical tradition in the Vedic and post-Vedic times alike. Most commonly, though, the term signifies the Sanskrit mental calculation Algorithm published in 1965 in a book entitled Vedic Mathematics by Professor Plofker as reconstructed from the Atharva-veda. These algorithms are not mentioned in traditional Vedic texts but they constitute an ingenious modern Sanskrit presentation of some mathematical ideas rather than the traditional source. In the books published in the last forty years on Indian mathematics, this confusion is addressed by many authors.

Many of the altar shapes involved simple symmetrical figures such as squares, rectangles, triangles, rhomboids and circles. Frequently, one such shape was required to be transformed into different one of the same size. Hence, the Sulba-Sutras rules often involve what we call area-preserving transformations of plane figures and thus include earliest known versions certain geometric formulae and constants. How this ritual geometry became integrated with the process of sacrificial offering is unknown. Did its mathematical rules emerge through attempts to represent cosmic entities physically and spatially in ritual? Or conversely, was existing geometric knowledge consciously incorporated into ritual practice to symbolize the Universal Truth or to induce "Satori" state of mind in the participants through perceptions of spatial relationship? I have not come across any explanation on this point. The best known Shulba-Sutras are attributed to four authors: Baudhayana, Manava, Apastamba, and Katyayana. According to some authors (Ref. 1 and 5), their contribution is judged on the basis of style and grammar of the language. One item is well established that Sulba-sutra of Kayayana appears to be the grammatical codification of Sanskrit by Panini in 400 B.C.

The Vedas and Astronomy

There has been a long debate whether the Vedic corpus, in addition to providing clues about general numeration practices and ritual geometry also preserves information about an ancient Indian tradition of Mathematical Astronomy. Since later Sanskrit mathematics is so often closely tied to astronomical texts, it would not be surprising if we found the two subjects linked in the Vedic times as well. Vedic texts prescribe periodic sacrifices to be performed at particular times such as the new full moon, solstices, and equinoxes. In the Rig-Veda, the year appears to be like to a twelve-spoke wheel that revolves round the heavens with 720 paired children, the days and nights within it. (Ref. 7). Quantitative astronomy requires some way of identifying positions in the heavens, usually with reference to particular fixed stars or group of stars. Named constellations are distinctly mentioned in some Vedic texts beginning with Yajur-Veda, specifically the band of 27 or 28 Nakshatras or Lunar Constellations., that lie in or near the path of the moon's monthly progress through the sky. The identification of a given point in the yearly liturgical cycle depended on what Nakshatras the moon or the sun occupied. At that time, so the sacrifice priests could keep track of where they were in the calendar by observing the positions of the sun and the moon with respect to the stars. At some point, the names of the twelve of these Nakshatras were applied to the twelve regular months to indicate the full moon appeared in that Nakshtras during that month. (Most of these names are still used in the Hindu calendar.

The Jyotisa-Vedanga

The earliest known mathematical exposition of astronomy and calenders, like its counterpart in the case of ritual geometry, is found not in the Vedic corpus itself but in its associated Vedanga. In the case of astronomy, the Vedanga is considered a single work in various forms known as Jyotisa-Vedanga .This text is the first available link between the ambiguous celestial calendric tables of the Vedas and the full blown Sanskrit mathematical astronomy of 1000 BC.

Mathematical Traces in the Early Classical Period

The middle of the first millennium B.C. is generally considered the approximate end of the Vedic period when the revealed scriptures were completed and Sanskrit started to shift from a primary language to a learned language. New research by Professors Bronkhorst in 2007 (handbook of oriental studies, section 2), however, suggests that parts of the Vedic corpus may be as much as several centuries younger, co-existing with Classical Sanskrit. Buddhism and Jainism emerged as distinct religious movements associated with the teachings of Buddha and Mahavir. In the next 200 years, Sanskrit was linguistically analyzed and standardized by the great grammarian, Panning, in the form that is now called classical Sanskrit., the first surviving document s in the Indo-Aryan language were inscribed, the incursion of the Alexander's armies spawned the first of the Indo-Greek kingdoms. There are very few remaining documents during the beginning of the Common Era (Year 0).

Pannini and formal scientific notation

A particularly important development in the history of Indian mathematics that was to have a profound impact on al mathematical treatises that followed the pioneering work by Pannini (6 century B.C.) in the field of Sanskrit Grammar and linguistics. Besides expounding a comprehensive and scientific theory of phonetics, phonology, and morphology, Panini provided the formal production of rules and definitions describing Sanskrit grammar in his treatise -Astadhyayi. Basic elements such as vowels, consonants, nouns and verbs were placed in classes. The construction of compound words and sentences were elaborated through ordered rules operating on underlying structures in a manner similar formal language theory. Today, Panning's construction can also be seen as comparable to modern definition of a mathematical function. G.G. Joseph (Ref. 1) speaks of the algebraic nature of Indian mathematics and how a consequence of the structure of the Sanskrit language arises. Ingermann's (Ref. 8) paper titled, "Panini Backus Form" finds Pnini's notation to be equivalent in its power to that of Backus –inventor of the Backus Normal Form used to describe the syntax of modern computer languages. Thus, Panini's original work provided an example of a scientific notation in characterizing algebraic equations and presenting algebraic theorems and results in a scientific format. Philosophical doctrines also had a profound influence on the development of mathematical concepts and formulations. Like the "Upnishadas" world view, space and time were considered limitless in Jain cosmology. This led to a very large numbers and definitions of infinite numbers. Jain mathematicians considered five different types of infinities: infinite in one direction, in two directions, in area, infinite everywhere and perpetually infinite. Permutations and combinations are listed in Bhagvat -Sutras (3000 B.C.) and Satanaga -Sutra (2000 B.C.).

Conclusion

The historical perspective presented here shows the full complexity of the Indian mathematical tradition and the extent to which its basic issues are still very incompletely understood. The question of what Indian mathematics was all about, and what made it a coherent intellectual discipline in the universe of Sanskrit learning and inspired particular paths of development, has been partially explored. A few examples of fundamental questions will give an idea of how much mystery still surrounds the subject:

A. What determined the major building- blocks or subjects of mathematics? For example, why did Mohair consider it possible in the Graniteware- Sangria to dispense with additions and subtractions of numbers as canonical arithmetic operations? How did the operation and procedures of the medieval arithmetic texts originate and how did a problem get assigned to a particular group?

B. How did the distinction between arithmetic and algebra develop?

C. How did ideas of proof develop over time? How much were they influenced by other branches of learning?

D. What, if any, was the role of foreign sources in Indian mathematics? How was it affected by Sanskrit purism or the goal of keeping Sanskrit Satraps as a part of sacred learning, separate from foreign knowledge outside the world of Dharma?

To the best of my knowledge, there are no answers to these questions. But one important discovery over these years is the development of Sanskrit and mathematics occurred together and lasted for 4000 years and made India the greatest country in the world. Unfortunately, Sanskrit is now a dead language and Indian mathematics became silent in about 1400 A.D.

References

1. Joseph G.G. The Crest of the Peacock. Princeton University Press. 2000.
2. Datta, B, and Singh, A. - History of Indian mathematics. A source book. 2 vols. Asia publishing Co. 1962.

3. Sir William Jones - Collected works Vol.3. 34-38, Lord Tignmouth - John Stockdale publication.
4. Plofker, K.- Mathematics in India, Princeton University Publication, 2009.
5. Murthy, P. Number symbolism in the Vedas, Electronic Journal of Vedic Studies, 12, Vol.3, 2005.
6. Seidenberg, A.—the origin of mathematics, 18, 1978. 301-342.
7. Kaks. – Indian Journal of History of Science, 35. 2000, 123-127.
8. Ingerman, P.Z. - Panini-Backus Form - Communications of the ACM 10, (3), 1967.

Chapter - 4

Famous Indian Mathematicians Brief Biographies

During the past few months, I collected many references with regard to the biographical sketches of famous Indian mathematicians who contributed and created the excellence in Indian mathematics. This article deals briefly with the biographies of some of the famous people.

The most fundamental contribution of ancient India in mathematics is the invention of decimal system of enumeration, including the invention of zero.

The decimal system uses nine digits (1 through 9) and the symbol Zero (for nothing) to denote all natural numbers by assigning a place value to the digits. The Arabs carried this system to Africa and Europe.

The Vedas and Valmiki Ramamyana used this system, though the exact dates of these works are not known. Mohenjo daro and Harappa excavations (about 3000B.C.) also give specimens of writing in India. Aryans came about 2000 B.C. and being very religious, they were mainly interested in planetary positions to calculate auspicious times, and they developed mathematics and astronomy towards this end. They identified various Nakshatras (constellations) and named the month after them. They could count up to 10^{22}. Values of irrational numbers such as “2 and “3 were also known to them to a high degree of approximation.

Pythagoras' theorem can also be traced to Aryan Sulbasutras. Jain used "10 as the value of " (circumference = " 10 × diameter). They were very fond of large numbers, and they classified numbers as enumerable and infinite. The Jains also worked out formulae for permutations and combinations, though this knowledge may have existed in Vedic times.

Bibliographies: Al the dates reported here are tentative except the recent ones.

1. Aryabhata (475 A.D.—550 A.D.) is the first well known Indian mathematician. Born in Kerala, he completed his studies at the University of Nalanda. In the section GANITA (Calculations) of his astronomical treatise Aryabhatia (499A.D.), he made the fundamental advance in finding the length of chords of circles, by using there half chord rather than the full chord used by the Greeks. He gave the value of as 3.1416, claiming for the first time, that it was an approximation, (He gave it in the form that the approximate circumference of a circle of diameter 20000 is 62832). He also gave methods of extracting square roots, summing arithmetic series, solving indeterminate equations, of the type.

$A x - b y = c$ and also added what is now known as the table of sines. He wrote a text book called Aryabhatasiddhanta. Even today, these data are used to prepare Hindu calendars (Panchangs) in recognition for his contribution to astronomy and mathematics, India's first satellite was named Aryabhata.

2. Brahmagupta (598– 665 A.D.) is renowned for introduction of negative numbers and operations on Zero into arithmetic. His main work was Brahmasphutasiddhanta which was a corrected version of old astronomical treatise Brahmasiddhanta. This work was translated into Arabic as Sind Hind. He formulated the rule of three and proposed rules for the solution of quadratic and simultaneous equations. He gave the formula for the area of a cyclic quadrilateral as A = " (s-a) (s-b) (s-c) (s-d) where s is the semi-perimeter. He was the first mathematician to treat algebra and arithmetic as two different branches of mathematics. He gave the solution of the indeterminate equation $N.X^{2} + 1 = y^{2}$. He is also the founder the branch of higher mathematics known as Numerical Analysis.

After Brahmagupta, the mathematician of some consequence was Sridhara, who wrote Patiganita Sara, a book on algebra, in 750A.D. Even Bhaskara refers to that work. After Sridhar, the most celebrated mathematician was Mahaviracharya or Mahavira. He wrote Ganita Sara Sangraha in 850A.D. which is the first book on Arithmetic in the present day form. He is the only Indian mathematician who has briefly referred to the ellipse (which he called Ayatvrit). The Greeks, by contrast, had studied conic sections in great detail.

3. Bhaskara (1114—1185 A.D.) or Bhaskaracharya is the most well-known ancient Indian mathematician. He was born in Bijapur, Karnataka in the Sahyadri Hills. He was the first to declare any number divided by zero is infinity and the sum of any number and infinity is also infinity. He is famous for his book Siddhanta Siromani (1150 A.D.). It is divided into four sections – Leelavati (Arithmetic), Bijaganita (algebra), Goladhayaya (sphere and celestial globe) and Grahagsnita (Mathematics of the planets). Leelawati was a very popular text book. Bhaskara introduced Chakrawal, or the cyclic method, to solve algebraic equations. Six centuries later, European mathematicians like Galois, Euler, and Lagrange rediscovered this method and called it "Inverse cycle". Bhaskara is also called the father of Differential Calculus. He also invented Differential coefficient and the basic idea of what is known as Rolle's Theorem. Unfortunately, none of the later Indian mathematicians did take notice of this enormous contribution. Five centuries later, Newton and Leibniz developed this subject. As an astronomer, Bhaskara is renowned for his concept of Tatkalikagati (instantaneous motion)

Well known mathematicians of the 20th Century

4. Srinivasa Ramanujan is undoubtedly the most famous Indian mathematical genius. He was born in a poor family at Erode, Tamilnadu, on Dec. 22, 1887. Largely self-taught, he feasted on Loney's trigonometry at the age of 13.

At the age of 15, his friends gave him Synopsis of Elementary results in pure and applied mathematics by George Carr. He used to write his ideas on loose sheets of paper. His three filled notebooks are now known as Ramanujan's Frayed Notebooks. Though he had no qualifying degree, the University of Madras granted him a monthly scholarship of Rs. 75 in 1913. A few months earlier, he had sent a letter to a great mathematician, Professor Hardy of Cambridge University in England in which he mentioned theorems and formulae for various differential equations. Hardy and his colleague, Littlewood immediately recognized his genius. Ramanujan sailed for Britain in 1914. Between 1914 and 1917, Ramanujan published 21 papers, some in collaboration with Hardy. His achievements include Hardy-Ramanujan –Littlewood Circle Method in Number Theory, Roger-Ramanujan's identities on partition of numbers, work on algebra of inequalities, elliptical functions, continued fractions, partial sums and products of Hypergeometric series etc. He was the second Indian to be elected as Fellow of the Royal Society in 1918. Later, he became the first Indian to be elected Fellow of Trinity College of Cambridge University. Ramanujan had intimate knowledge and familiarity with numbers. During his illness in a hospital in Cambridge, Professor Hardy came to visit him. Hardy remarked that he had taken the taxi with a number 1729, a singularly exceptional number. Ramanujan immediately responded that this number is absolutely unique number and is the smallest integer that can be represented in two ways as the sum of

$$1729 = 1^3 + 12^3 = 9^3 + 10^3$$

Ramanujan was suffering from tuberculosis and had to return to India in 1919 and he died in April 26, 1920.

5. P.C. Mahalnobis: He was a brilliant statistician and founded the Indian Statistical Research Institute in Calcutta. In 1958, he started the National Sample Survey which gained international fame. Mahalnobis is also known as an advisor to Prime Minister Jawaharlal Nehru and as the co-founder of the historical Five Year Plans (I became familiar with his work because my dissertation in the business was written on the first five year plan).

6. C.R. Rao: A well-known statistician, famous for his "Theory of Estimation" (1945). His formulae and theory include "Cramer-Rao inequality", "Fischer-Rao Theorem."

7. D.R. Karpekar L 1905-1988) is well known for as the inventor of "Karpekar Constant" 6174. Take any four digit number in which all

digits are not alike. Arrange the digits in descending order and subtract form it the number formed by arranging the digits in ascending order. If this process is repeated with reminders, ultimately number 6174 is obtained, which then generates itself.

8. Harish Chandra (1923-1983) developed the Infinite Dimensional Group representation theory.

9. Narendra Karmarkar: While working at Bell Lab. near Princeton University, New Jersey in 1984, he developed the new Algorithm to solve Linear programming problems. This was used to solve the complex calculations in a much easier and faster way and had many immediate applications in various fields such as communications etc.

Famous Mathematicians in the last 10 years

10. Chandrakant Khare: Becoming well known for his extraordinary work on

"Fermat Theorem"

11. Divakar Vishwanathan: In 1999, he wrote a paper about Diwakar's constant which is the Limit Of The Ratio of Consecutive Random Fibonacci numbers. There is a lot of discussion on this and some prominent mathematicians are calling this constant as the Golden Ratio. I am keeping a close watch in some journals for further developments.

I may have missed some names and will do some corrections as time goes by. All the dates before the year 1800 are approximate since most of these dates are being revised as new research shows a good deal of discrepancy with the recorded data.

History of Indian Mathematics Needs A Revision

History is defined as the aggregate of a record of narrative description of past events. A well written history describes the continuum of events in succession leading from the past to the present and even into the future.

In my opinion, the history of Indian mathematics as recorded or written does not follow this systematic arrangement of facts. There are many reasons and some research is required to ascertain and correct some important facts.

In the past few weeks, I was trying to write a chronology of well-known Indian mathematician's bibliography so I can try to find the date of his invention to link into a cohesive story to explain the reasons for excellence in Indian mathematics. There are many cases where the data are conflicting. I will provide some important cases.

Case 1: Aryabhata is also known as Aryabhata 1 to distinguish him from the later mathematician of the same name who lived 400 years later. An early historian called Al-Beruni (Ref. 1) has not helped in understanding Aryabhata's life, for he seemed to believe there were two Aryabhatas living at the same time. He therefore, created confusion of two people of the same name which was not clarified until 1926 when B.Dutta (Ref. 2) pointed that Al-Beruni's two Aryabhatas were one and the same person.

Case 2: Compare Hash (Ref.3, page 342) and Kak (Ref. 4, page 328), the former follows the mainstream opinion placing the emergence of quantitative astronomy in Vedic India in 2000 B.C., while the latter suggests it goes back as far as 4000B.C. Why is the difference by 2000 years?

Case 3: There is willful mix-up of Chandragupta Maurya (1534-1500 B.C.) And Chandragupta (327-320 B.C.) of the Gupta dynasty, by making the former a similar age with Alexander, the Great and by erasing the latter's reference altogether. More than that, the entire chronology of events was shortened by more than 1200 years. Consequently, the times of ancient astronomers and mathematicians had to be moved into the Christian era.

Case 4: Max Mueller, an ambitious and influential Indologist, came up the age of Rig Veda to be 1200 B.C. with the stipulation that it was written by nomadic Aryans (riding on horseback, presumably, with a mobile library). Actually, the Rig Veda was compiled well before 3000 B.C. (Ref. 4).

I came across many cases like these and I do not see any need to elaborate.

Background of Analysis

Why is it so hard to find information about Indian math? I have seen many articles asking this plain question at one time or another. Usually a question like this is posed by a frustrated researcher engaged in some attempt to integrate the Indian tradition into the history of mathematical sciences elsewhere in the world.

There are many reasons for this discrepancy in historical facts. There is no denying the fact that Indian tradition presents some unique challenges. Indians are poor in writing history. This is true not only in the subject of mathematics but in almost every subject I can think of. It is not that information about the subject is not available but it is very difficult to separate reliable information from speculation or pure invention. In a recent article (Ref. 5), the authors complain bitterly about the "Eurocentric historical differences" towards the Indian documented treasures. For example, we are told the Gregory –Leibniz series for P/4 was first discovered by Nilkanta and was clearly stated in his Tantra Sangrhra (1500 A.D.). The so-called Pythagoras theorem (600 B.C.) and its converse were known to the Indian mathematicians about 3000 B.C. The general principle of trigonometric functions was enunciated in Surya Siddhanta preceding even the Sulvasutras period. Brahmagupta (30 B.C.) solved the second order indeterminate question NX +1= Y2 and foresaw Newton's law of gravitation. The authors demonstrated that Bhaskara 2 (486 B.C.) invented Differential Calculus which was systematized by Newton and Leibniz in late 17th century. The Greeks got their plain geometry from India.

When do you think all these new discoveries come to light? This was all in the last 30 years and well recorded by Lakshmikanthan and Leela (Ref.5). In modern times, it is not fashionable to pay tributes to the old country while enjoying the riches of the adopted country. (I am one of them but trying very hard to break that habit). It is necessary to note the Universities of Nagarjuna, Takshila, Tamraparni, Vallabhi, Vikramasilla were internationally reputed and gracefully functioned for a long time but eventually perished many years before Oxford, Cambridge, Sorbonne and Goettingen had their days. We say they were perished but according the recent history (Ref.5), they were made to perish by invading Barbarians. Very strange to say, but all this is very recent information with the precise dates and correct information to the best of our knowledge. The Indian historians should be able to construct a reasonable narrative for the history of Indian mathematics based on the available and new data and plausible references.

As I understand, the earliest recorded history of mathematics takes us back to 4000-3000 B.C. and was written in early form of Sanskrit. Their earliest surviving texts mostly reflect basic mathematical knowledge supporting a simple ritual calendar and the economy of a pastoral society. In about 1000 to 500 B.C., Sanskrit texts began to show more sophisticated techniques in geometry for religious ritual and astronomy. Now, it is believed that the latter subject was influenced from Mesopotamia. Over the next few hundreds of years, the Indian Mathematical sciences flourished as one of the richest and most fascinating scientific tradition as ever known .Using rules composed mostly in Sanskrit verse and detailed prose commentaries on them, and without the formal deductive proof structure that we know today. THIS WAS ONE BIG FACTOR WHY THE WESTERN MATHEMATICIANS DID NOT CONSIDER INDIAN MATHEMATICS SERIOUSLY. The mathematical knowledge of India has long been recorded as excellent and extraordinarily rich. The European scholars, who encountered Indian mathematics in the 17 and 18th centuries, were often completely at sea concerning the ages of the texts, their interrelationship, and even their identities. The sheer number of such works and the uncertainty surrounding the most basic chronology of Sanskrit literature gave rise to great confusion. To top all this, a lot of valuable literature was purposely destroyed, burned by the invaders over a number of years. This led to even greater confusion. Another factor also played a very big part. The European historians purposely minimized and altered the history they knew because they wanted to show the superiority of Western culture over the Asian culture.

In my opinion, the history of Indian mathematics as we know today does not tell the facts and lot of fundamental research is required to know all the facts. This would take a number of years. A good start has already been made. Hope it continues.

References

1. Joseph, G. G. The Crest of the Peacock. Princeton University Press 2000.
2. Data, B. and Singh, A.N. –A history of Hindu Mathematics, Asia Publishing House 1962.
3. Hash, Yukio –Remarks on the Indo-Tibetan astronomy, page 341-369. This was reported by Professor Plofker, Princeton University Press 2009.
4. Kak, Subhash, -Birth and development of Indian astronomy, Page 303-340 2000.
5. Lakshmikanthan, V. and Leela, S.—The Origin of mathematics, University Press of America 2005.

Chapter - 5

The Importance of Mathematical Logic

Introduction

In mankind's eternal quest to understand the World around him, he has always turned to a select set of essential elements to gain knowledge of the World. Among the most important ones are language, mathematics and philosophy which have been recognized by philosophers across the world as three crucial components in our attempt to grasp that which we call Reality. Throughout history, we have attempted to understand, define, and communicate these concepts of reality through this framework. All conscious thoughts of mathematics and philosophy are conveyed through a language. The importance of language to philosophy has recently been enumerated through various methods. Similarly, the need of mathematics to philosophy is discussed in depth through logic and that is the prime reason mathematical logic is the science which is vital for all of us to understand.

The Story of Mathematics

The history of mathematics is nearly as old as humanity itself. Since antiquity, mathematics has been fundamental to advances in science, engineering and philosophy. It has evolved from simple counting, measurements and calculations and the systematic of the shapes and forms and motions of physical objects, through application of abstraction, imagination and most importantly, logic.

From the notched bones of early man to the mathematical advances brought about by settled agriculture in Ancient India and Mesopotamia and the reactionary developments of Ancient Greece and its Hellenistic empire, the story of mathematics is a long and impressive one.

The East carried on the baton, particularly by the Indian and Sumerian people before the focus of mathematical innovation moved to Europe in the late Middle Ages and the Renaissance. Then, a whole new series of revolutionary developments occurred in the 17th and the 18th centuries Europe, setting the stage for the increasing complexity and abstraction of the 19th century mathematics and finally the audacious and sometimes devastating discoveries of the 20th century.

My major intention is to bring about the tremendous contribution made by important thinkers to our understanding of some logical conclusions.

Eastern Logic

It is believed in the West that logic began with Aristotle, and that logic is universal. The core of the Western thought— including present day formal Mathematics and the philosophy of Science—is premised on the belief that logical truths are universal, that they are necessary truths and that logical deduction is certain and infallible. These beliefs about logic, however, are untenable, both historically and philosophically, in larger picture which takes the non-Western account.

Philosophically, present day formal logic, like the 12th century text, Organon, attributed to Aristotle, supposes that deduction relates to two-valued logic. In such a logic, an affirmation A conjoined with its negative (-A) makes a contradictory pair, which any conclusion B can be valid inferred by the rule of Inference known as Reductio ad Absurdum. Two examples, one for and the second one against are already cited to make the argument absurd.

However, the various logics used for interference in India, prior to even the historical Aristotle, were neither two-valued nor even truth-functional.

The Digha Nikaya provides an example as Buddha explains in the Brahmajala Sutta, there are four alternatives:

1. The world in finite - first case
2. The world is not finite - second case

3. The World is both finite and infinite - third case
4. The world is neither finite or infinite - fourth case
5. There are no other cases.

The semantic interpretation of the third case is that the world may be finite in one direction, but infinite in another. To me, this presents no absurdity, and could conceivably be in the nature of things. I personally prefer the third case.

The meaning of the fourth case, not so well brought out in the English translation of the Digha Nikaya, may be better understood as follows: Consider a person who refuses to take a position, and denies that he affirms any of the first three cases above. His position can be described by the Fourth Case.

The need for such a forth case is apparent from the Thinking then prevalent. Likewise, the absence of any further cases is a reference to further negations used by pre-Buddhist thinkers like Sanjaya, the skeptic who tried to wriggle out of even fourth position and whose comprehensive refusal to take any position was described by the Buddha as being like the

"wriggling of the eel".

These four cases are systematically issued by later-day Buddhist thinkers like Nagarjuna and who taught at the University of Nalanda (India). The latter developed a theory of (logical) quantifiers, 'for all' etc. based on this sort of logic. From the perspective of present – day formalist treatments of logic, it should be noted that Buddhist logic is not multi-valued but is rather a quasi-truth-functional logic.

History of Mathematical Logic

As stated earlier, logic is the formal systematic study of the principles of valid references and reasoning. Logic is used in most intellectual activities of philosophy and mathematics. In short, it takes general forms which argument may take, which forms are valid and which are fallacies. This is a very good reason why mathematical logic is extensively studied in new science like Computer Science and Engineering.

The basic principles of logic and its use in mathematics were well understood by the philosophers and mathematicians of the classical Greek era, and Aristotle provided the first systematic written treatment of Logic. His description of Logic was carried out in the context of natural language.

And it is considered Informal rather than Symbolic. It was not until a thousand years later that the seeds of modern mathematical logic were sown, with Aristotle's work as a basis. In the late 1600's Gottfried Leibniz—the famous German mathematician and one of the co-inventors of Calculus along with Sir Isaac Newton, expressed and worked toward the goal of creating a symbolic language of Reasoning that could be used to solve all well-defined problems, not just in mathematics but in science as well.

Almost two more centuries passed before Augustus De Morgan and George Boole extended Leibniz's work and began to create Modern Symbolic Language. As much as I know, De Morgan is best remembered for the two laws of Propositional Logic that bear his name, while Boolean Algebra found many uses in the 20th century, essentially, the designs of the Computer Circuitry. Finally, Predicate Logic as we know today was created in late 1800's by Gottlieb Frege and few years later by Giuseppe Peano. Both were involved in the formulation of the modern day Mathematical Logic.

There were, however, some contradictions in their reasoning and mathematics. A monumental effort was made Bertrand Russell and Alfred North Whitehead which they published in Principia Mathematica in two volumes which perfected the mistakes and made the entire subject of mathematical logic fairly popular. This has become the principle subject in Computer Science.

In an examination of the work done by mathematical logic, we may consider either the mathematical results, the method of mathematical reasoning as revealed by modern work or the intrinsic nature of mathematical propositions according to the analysis of Bertrand Russell. It is impossible to distinguish exactly these three aspects of the subject, but over the last few years, there is enough of distinction to serve the purpose of a framework for discussion. My lack of knowledge of higher level of mathematics does not allow me to go into deep discussion but to the best of my knowledge, a lot of work is presently going on.

From the philosophical point of view, the most brilliant results are the exact theories which we have been able to form about Infinity and Continuity. It is now believed that the number of an infinite collection is equal to the number of a part of this collection.

After what has been written in this article so far, it is easy to see what must be thought about the intrinsic nature of propositions of pure mathematics. As much as I know, in pure mathematics, we never have to discuss facts that are applicable to such and such an individual object; we need never know anything about the actual world. We are concerned exclusively with variables, that is to say, with any subject, about which hypotheses are made which may be fulfilled sometimes, but whose verification is only necessary for the importance of the deductions and not for their truth.

Mathematics, therefore, is wholly composed of propositions which contain variables and logical constants, that is to say, purely formal propositions for the logical constants which constitute form for some interpretation. As much as we know today, human knowledge is divided into two kinds: Knowledge of particular facts, which alone allows us to affirm existence, and knowledge of logical truths which alone allows us to reason about data. In our daily lives, the two kinds of knowledge are intermixed: the propositions which are affirmed are obtained from particular premises by means of logical principles.

To conclude, we have seen, in the first place, that mathematical logic has resolved the problems of infinity and continuity, and that it has made possible a solid philosophy of Space, Time, and Motion. In the second place, we have seen that pure mathematics can be defined as the class of propositions which are expressed exclusively in terms of variables and logical constants.

Chapter - 6

Ancient Indian Mathematics - A New Version

Introduction

Recently, I came across three remarkable books on Ancient Indian Mathematics. The first two are written by Professor Agathe Keller of Germany and the third by Professor David Pingree of Harvard University (Ref. 1, 2 and 3). These books put the entire mathematical development of ancient India in a proper historical sense with corresponding evidence from Sanskrit literature. This article gives a different perspective and background of origin and success of mathematics in ancient India.

Indian Mathematics

This mathematics emerged from ancient times until the end of the 18th century had its beginning in the Bronze age Indus Valley civilization (2600-1900 B.C.) and the Iron age Vedic culture (1500-500 B.C.). In the classical period of Indian mathematics, (400 – 1200 A.D.), important contributions were made by scholars like Aryabhata, Brahmagupta, and Bhaskara. 2.

Indian mathematicians made early contributions to the study of the Decimal number system, Zero, Negative numbers, Arithmetic, and Algebra. In addition, Trigonometry, having evolved in the Hellenistic world and introduced into ancient India through translation of Greek works, was further advanced in India and in particular, the modern definitions of Sine and Cosine were developed.

These mathematical concepts were transmitted to the Middle East, China, and later To Europe.

The Oral Mathematical Tradition

Ancient and medieval Indian mathematical works, all composed in Sanskrit, usually consisted of a section of Sutras in which a set of rules or problems were stated with great economy in Verse in order to aid in memorization by a student. This was followed by a second section consisting of a Prose commentary (sometimes multiple commentaries by different scholars) that explained the problem in more detail and provided justification for the solution.

In the prose section, the form (and therefore its memorization) was not considered as important as the ideas involved. All Mathematical works were Orally Transmitted until approximately 500 B.C. Thereafter, they were transmitted both orally and in manuscript form.

A later landmark in Indian mathematics was the development of the series exponential trigonometric functions (sine, cosine and arc tangent) by the mathematicians in the 15th century.

Styles of Memorization

Prodigious energy was expended by ancient Indian culture in ensuring that these texts were transmitted from generation to generation with inordinate fidelity. For a memorization of the sacred Vedas included up to eleven forms of recitation of the text. The texts were subsequently "Proof-Read" by different recited forms of recitation included the "JA –TA-PA-THA" (literally mesh recitation) in which every adjacent words in the text were first recited in their original order, then repeated in reverse order, and finally repeated in the original order. The recitation proceeded as:

Word1 Word2, Word2 Word1, Word1 Word2; Word 2 Word3 And So On.

In another form of recitation, DVAJA-PA-THA (literally flag recitation), a sequence of words were recited and memorized by paving the first two and the and the last two words as:

Word1 Word2, Word (N-1) Word N; Word2 Word3;

Word (N-3) Word (N-2) And So On;

The most complex form of recitation, ***Ghana-patha (Literally Dense Recitation) took the form:***

Word1word2, Word2word 1, Word1 Word2 Word3, Word3 Word2 Word1word2 Word3, Word 3 Word2 Word3 Word4 Word3 Word2, Word2 Word3 Word4 and so on:

That these methods have been effective is testified to by the preservation of the Ancient Religious Text, the RIGVEDA (can, 1500 B.C.) as a single text. Similar methods were used for memorizing mathematical formulae whose transmission remained literally ORAL until the end of the Vedic period (500 B.C.) (Personal Note: In all these years of reading books on various subjects, I never came across such a ingenious way of learning the very basics of our daily living).

The Sutra Genre

Mathematical activity in Ancient India began as a part of "Methodological Reflection" on the sacred Vedas, which took the form of works called "VEDANGAS" or Ancillaries Veda.

(7-4th centuries B.C.). The need to conserve the sound of sacred text SIKSA (phonetics) and CHANDAS (metrics); to conserve the meaning of by the use of the Vyasas (grammar) or Nikuta (etymology) and to correctly perform the rites at the use of Kalpa (ritual) and JYOTISA (astronomy) gave rise to the six disciplines called VEDANGAS. Mathematics arose as a part of the last two disciplines.

Vedic Period: (1500- 400 B.C.)

The religious texts of the Vedic Period provide evidence for the use of large numbers during the time of the last Veda, the YAJURVEDASAMHITA (1200-900B.C.), numbers as large as possible being included in the texts. For example, the MANTRA (sacrificial formula) invokes power numbers from hundred to a trillion. "Hail to SATA (10^2), hail Sahaasra (10^3), hail to Ayuta (10 4), hail to Niyuta (10 5), hail to Prayuta (10 6), hail to Arbuda (10 7), hail to Nyarbuda (10 8), hail to Samudra (10 9), a literally ocean, hail to Madhya

(10 10), hail to Anta (hundred billion (10 11). This system goes on until a trillion is reached.

The Satapatha Brahmana (9th centuries B.C.) contains rules for ritual geometric construction that are similar to the Sulba Sutras. The Sub sutras list rules for the construction of sacrificial fire altars. I will not go into details here but the entire setup for the details calculation is quite impressive.

According to Hayashi (Page 363, ref. 4) the Sulba sutras contain "the earliest extraordinary expression of the Pythagorean Theorem in the world, although it had already been covered by the old Babylonians.

Jain Mathematics: (400 B.c.—200 A.d.)

Although Jainism as a religion and philosophy predates its most famous exponent, Mahavira (6th century B.C.) Who was a contemporary of Gautum Buddha? Most texts on mathematical topics were composed after the 6th century B.C. The Jain mathematicians were considered very important historically as crucial links between the mathematicians of the Vedic period and that of the "Classical" period.

A significant contribution of the Jain mathematicians lay in their freeing mathematics from its religious and ritualistic constraints. In particular, their fascination with very large numbers and infinities, led them to classify large numbers in three classes: Enumerable, Innumerable, and Infinite. Not content with a simple infinity, they went on to define five different types of infinity: the infinite in one direction, infinite in two directions, the infinite in area, infinite everywhere, infinite perpetually. In addition, the Jain mathematicians devised notations for simple power (exponents) of numbers like squares, cubes which enabled them to define algebraic equations.

Pingala

Among other scholars of this period who contributed to mathematics, the most famous was Pin gala, (300-200 B.C.), a musical theorist who authored CHANDRA SHASTRA, a Sanskrit treatise. There is a lot of evidence in his work of PASCAL TRIANGLE and

Binomial coefficients, although the proof of Binomial Theorem is missing. Pingala also worked on the basic ideas of Fibonacci Numbers. There are a lot of details which I do not need to illustrate in this article. Suffice to say, Pingala's extensive work was absolutely amazing.

Numerals And Decimal Number System

The earliest extant script used in India was the Karachi script used in the North West. It is thought to be of Aramaic origin (the language spoken by Jesus Christ and his followers). This script had the synopsis of symbols and numeral systems, which were initially not based on a place-value. The first database evidence of the use of the Decimal System in India (ca.270 A.D.) of Sphuidhavja, a versification of an earlier Indian prose adaptation of a lost Hellenistic Astrology.

The Classical Period (400-1200 A.d.)

I do not want to add more here because I have written a lot of articles in my Book 1. Just to emphasize, this period covers the works of Aryabhata, Varahamihira, Brahmagupta, Bhaskara 1 and Bhaskara 2. Their work gives a wide and a broad shape in many branches of mathematics.

Fifth And Sixth Centuries:

Though the authorship is unknown, the SURYA SIDDHANTA (ca.400 A.D.) contains the records of modern TRIGONOMETRY. Due to a large number of foreign words in the documents, eminent historians have concluded the roots are in Mesopotamia and Greece. These documents show the Trigonometric functions for the first time:

- Sine (Jya)
- Cosine (Konya)
- Inverse Sine (Okra jay)

It also contains the earliest uses of:

- Tangent
- Secant

The Hindu Cosmological time explained in the text, which were copied, gives. The Average length of the Sidereal year is 365.2563627 days which is 5 seconds longer than 365.3563629 days.

Later, Aryabhata made references to this text and translated in Arabic and Latin.

Kerala Mathematics (1300-1600 A.d.)

I do not intend to go into detail because it is well covered in my Book 1. Just to highlight, the Kerala school of Astronomy

And Mathematics was founded by MADHAVA of Sengama gram in Kerala and included among its members: Neelkantha Somayajii, Jyasthadeva, Achyuta, Pishrati, Malpatghur Narayana. This school flourished between 14th and 16th centuries.

Charges of Eurocentrism

It has been suggested that Indian contribution to Mathematics have not been given acknowledgement in modern history and that many discoveries and inventions of mathematicians are presently attributed to their Western counterparts. According to G.G. Joseph (Ref. 5), their work takes on board some of the objections raised about the class of European trajectory. The awareness of (Indian and Arabic mathematics) is too likely to be tempered with dismissive rejections of their importance compared to Greek mathematics. The contribution from other civilizations most notably, China and India are perceived either as borrowers from Greek sources or having made only minor contributions to mainstream mathematical development. Openness to more recent research findings, especially, in the case of Indian mathematics is sadly missing.

The historian of mathematics, Florian Cajori (Ref. 6), suggests that Diaphantus got his first glimpse of algebraic knowledge from India. More recently, as discussed in the above sections, the Infinite series of Calculus, Trigonometric functions, (rediscovery by Gregory, Taylor and Maclaurin in the 20th century) were described with proofs in India by mathematicians of the Kerala School remarkably two centuries earlier. Some scholars have recently suggested knowledge of these results were transmitted to Europe from Kerala by traders and Jesuit Missionaries in 1500 A.D. Both Indian and Arab scholars made discoveries before the 17th century of a considerable part of Calculus. However, they were not able to, as Newton did, to combine many differing ideas under the two, unifying themes of the differentiation and integral, show the connection between the two and turn Calculus into a problem-solving tool we know today.

Today, there are many scholars working on the subject of Ancient Indian mathematics and more will be written as time goes by. From my personal point of view, this is a remarkable subject and it has been my proud heritage to pursue it to the best of my ability.

References

1. Keller, Agathe (2006), Expounding the Mathematical Seed. Vol 1: The translation of Bhaskara1: Berlin, Berkhauser Verlag 172 pages.
2. Keller, Agathe (2006), expounding the mathematical seed. Vol. 2: The Translation of Bhaskara.
3. Pingree, David (1978) The Yavanajataka of Sphujidhavja, edited by D. Pingree, Harvard Oriental Studies.
4. Hayashi, Takao (1965) Indian Mathematics –Johns Hopkins University Press
5. Joseph, G.G. (2000) The Crest of the Peacock; The Non-European roots of Indian mathematics, Princeton University Press.
6. Cajori, Florian (1893) The Hindus, A history of mathematics, page 86 - McMillan and company.

Chapter - 7

Is a Science of History Possible?

Introduction

The Empire unified all the civilizations at last. After generations of war, the last enemies have been defeated. Citizens of the empire can, it seems, look forward to a permanent peace and prosperity. But a maverick mathematician named Hari Seldon has disturbing news. His new science of Psychohistory, built from equations that integrate the actions of myriads of individuals predicts large scale social trends. The equations foretell the decay and eventual collapse of the central power, rebellions by regional barons, rogue generals and finally a bitter civil war that will transform the capital into a ghost town. The decline and fall of the empire over the ensuing centuries unfolds precisely as the humble mathematician said it would.

This scenario from the "Foundation Trilogy of Isaac Asimov" occurs in the future on the planet Trantor, the capital of a mighty Galactic Empire. In Asimov's fantasy, human history can be understood and predicted in the same way which physicists understand and predict the trajectories of the planets. The key to the prediction of human societies is Psychohistory, the branch of mathematics that deals with the reactions of human conglomerates to fixed social and economic stimuli. The ability of Psychohistories to make accurate forecasts is, however, not absolute. Psycho history cannot predict the actions of a single individual. But it can predict collective behaviors. As Hari Seldon explains "By knowledge, your freedom of action would be expanded and the number of additional variables introduced would become greater then mathematics can handle."

Asimov's trilogy captured the imagination of lots of readers including many scientists and historians. For centuries, philosophers have considered over the scientific study of history. Despite some dissenting voices, the consensus has been that scientific study of human societies is impossible because they differ too much from physiological and biological systems. They consist not of simple identical particles such as atoms and molecules but of human individuals, each unique, endowed with free will and capable of purposeful actions. The verdict has been that any sort of scientific history must remain scientific fiction rather than real science. I think this is for the best.

A science of history sounds cold and hard – wouldn't it destroy our enjoyment of the wonderfully rich tapestry of the past. On a darker side, might not such a science enable some nasty fellow to manipulate societies to a nefarious purpose? Sometimes, I wonder the history of India during 11th century would have changed considerably had science and history acted together to save the glories of India rather than giving way to the invading ruffians. What a awful shame that Isaac Asimov and Hari Seldon were not born to warn the Indian kings of the impending disaster that could last for centuries.

In spite of all the troubles, we have not ceased to enjoy the blue sky of a brilliant summer day or the play of colors in a glorious sunset. After all, the physicists, beginning with Indian astronomers worked out exactly how the colors of the sky result from the interaction of sunlight with the atmosphere.

Here, I would like to address the question raised by Asimov and other people before him including Karl Marx and Leo Tolstoy. Is Science of History possible? Can we design a theory for the collapse of mighty empires that would be worse than, say, our understanding of earthquakes. They can make limited predictions as to which areas of earth are likely to be hit next day by an earthquake. Can science of history similarly explain why states crumble and perhaps, which societies are in danger of collapse?

Empire Building

Why did some initially small and insignificant nations go on to build mighty empires? Can we understand how imperial powers rise and fall? An empire is a large, multi-ethnic, territorial state with a complex power structure. The key variable is the size.

Historians like Arnold Toynbee wrote volumes on the rise and fall of whole civilizations, others have been fascinated with the spread of religions, art of styles, progress in science and technology etc.

The very stability and internal peace that strong empires impose contain within them the seeds of future chaos. Stability and internal peace bring prosperity and population increase. Demographic growth leads to overpopulation which in turn causes lower wages, higher land rents, and falling per capita incomes for the commoners. Declining standards of life breed discontent and strife.

The task of the historian of science is to study the origins and historical course of science, both in its theoretical development and in its external relations with the society within which it existed.

In other words, the historians work is not a matter of establishing certain facts about historical events confirming certain demonstrable casual connection, but also a process of entering into an intellectual world of a particular period.

In the Positivist tradition, the ambition was primarily to "understand science itself", its hypotheses, and conditions; a more externalist approach attaches more importance to the understanding of history and with it the past played by science during different periods. The emphasis shifts from science as we see it today for a particular historical period in which science was an important or unimportant factor. But if we are able to understand and analyze the function of science, we have to understand its origin and its structure. Theories do not arise by spontaneous generation - - they develop in continuous interaction with other theories and the world of ideas, prejudices and policies which exist at that time. The task of the historian is, therefore, not only to understand but also to reconstruct, to build up different possible worlds. Such a possible world need not be global but the underlying philosophy must not be too restricted in scope, or relevant only to certain parts of more complex theories or to theories explaining very limited phenomena.

Concluding Remarks

In the last few weeks, I spent a considerable time to research on my latest article: Ancient Indian Mathematics - A new Revision. I was very proud of the achievements of Indian mathematics and then it occurred to me the fate of India after the 11th century was not the same. The country's fortune went from glorious days to a colonial status which lasted for 900 years. God is money and we worship the new god as if there is no end. India has to think as one unified country with lot of social interchange and only Hari can bring this about.

Otherwise, India will repeat the cycle in a short time.

The Silent Era (or the Demise) of the Indian Mathematics

(1600 A.D. -present)

It has been established that many of the key results of mathematics, some of which are the very "core" of modern day mathematics are of Indian origin. The results are almost all independently "rediscovered" by European scholarsduring and after the

"Renaissance" and while remarkable, history should be complete and to neglect facts is ignorant and arrogant.

A Brief History of Indian Mathematics

Indian mathematics made great strides in developing Arithmetic, Algebra, Geometry, Infinite Series expansions and Calculus. A chronology of well-known contributors is attached at the end of this article. All this work was remarkable because it occurred so much earlier (4000 B.C — 1400A.D.) that is, advanced mathematical ideas were developed by people culturally and academically advanced than the Europeans. This comment can be controversial but there are instances where the contributions by Indian mathematicians were neglected (Ref. 1&2).

Advances by Indian mathematicians continued in so-called Kerala Mathematics Period (1400-1600 A.D.). After that period, the contributions by Indian mathematicians were not of high standard and as significant as compared to the earlier period. This was the Silent Era and / or the Demise of the Indian mathematics from 1600 to the present day. To understand this unusual absence of activity, I read many books and articles by Indian and European scholars and unfortunately, did not come across any article written by an Indian scholar who did any analysis of this problem. The only critical analyses were written by either Scottish or English mathematical historians which is strange. More on this subject is in later. In the following pages, I analyze and seek to understand the causes which led to the problem.

Analysis Of The Silent Era

It seems the main reasons for the neglect of Indian mathematics are the combination of Religious, Cultural and psychological make ups of the predominantly Hindu society. Alternately, the society can also be referred to as Sanskrit society. P. Rasheed (Ref. 3) mentions this period as the conflict between modernism and tradition. There were powerful forces at work that inhibited the growth of mathematics and science in India. In my understanding, there were three main problems. Let us analyze each problem:

1. Moslem Invasion of India (1100 A.D. to 1700 A.D.)

Since 1100 A.D., India was repeatedly attacked and invaded by the Moslems from the north. The establishment of Islamic military and political control over the northern part of India started in about 1100A.D. This began as looting expeditions conducted by the Ghaznavi sultans from Afghanistan. From the early sultans to the 1600, a succession of Moslem invaders controlled the city of Delhi and the surrounding regions. In 1526, the central Asian ruler known as Babur, a descendant of Timurkhan seized Delhi and initiated the Mughal Empire which lasted until the middle of the 1700's when the British annexed it. The Indo-Moslem Empire changed many aspects of the Indian life, especially in the northern part of the country. Constant wars between the native population and the invaders took a heavy toll on the stability and prosperity of many Indians. Military conquests of a local kingdom often involved the looting and desecration of important temples sacred to Hindus, Buddhists and Jains were destroyed sometimes to accompaniments of militant monotheistic rhetoric attacking polytheistic beliefs and practices. The immense waste of lives and various resources must have inflicted great and semi-permanent damages to the state of learning including mathematical knowledge.

It would be a severe distortion to assume that the Indo-Moslem era consisted of antagonism and violence. Under the Mughal emperor, Akbar, in the 16th Century, promoted religious balance and took interest in non-Moslem (Hindu and Jain) learning. Unfortunately, this quiet did not last more than 100 years. In the overall tragedy, the well-established schools of mathematics did not survive. No numbers are available.

The efforts of a more comprehensive assimilation of Islamic mathematical science launched in the courts of Delhi and Jaipur apparently did not make much impression on the Indians outside of those cosmopolitan elite settings. In fact, some Hindu scholars viewed foreign technical innovations with strong distrust as potentially damaging to the "Purity" of the traditional Hindu knowledge (Ref. 1).

2. The End of Traditional way of Learning

The role of mathematics and mathematicians in pre-modern Indian society is potentially a vast subject that is still poorly understood. How many people were engaged in mathematical pursuits? How did they earn their living? What were their social goals and their social status? Most importantly, how did they perpetuate their professional accomplishments and mathematical knowledge from one generation to the next? These questions involve the very "core" of the Indian or Sanskrit society fundamentals and are not well understood even today.

I did not come across any reference where I could find answers too many questions. As I understand, more research is now going on this subject.

In the following paragraphs, I derived information from the autobiographical details presumably obtained from pedagogical tradition (Ref. 2&4). But the data seldom go beyond some sub-sets of the following:

1. The author himself
2. The hereditary social groups to which he belonged
3. his father and other relatives
4. His teacher
5. His place of residence, birth and family origin
6. His royal or noble patron
7. His favorite deity

In addition to these facts, the caste system in the classical Sanskrit period became much more complex and rigid. Its inflexibility was stressed in many writings of some mathematicians (Ref. 5). Bearing in mind these various caveats, I have made the following generalizations about the teachers and learners of Indian (Sanskrit) mathematics. Among the Hindus, astronomer-mathematicians were exclusively Brahmans (Hindus of the highest caste) pursuing the subject. The education involved the individual study with a teacher in the same area. Over the number of years, many learned families accumulated large libraries of manuscripts which enriched the studies of future generations. Currently, many Indian regional traditions of mathematical practice including vernacular primer texts teaching basic numeric are being studied by many researchers. (Ref.5)

There also existed some educational institutions larger than the family tutorials and the local schools. There are many references I came across that the temples, monasteries and other institutions where many Hindus and Jains studied. If the internal structure still contains many mysteries, so does the external structure with respect to other genres of Sanskrit literature. Perhaps, it was one sided: mathematical texts were grounded in the basics of Sanskrit disciplines such as grammar and logic .From the early 1300, the increasing interaction between Indian mathematics and the Moslem rule and Arabic mathematicians complicated the entire basis of learning and the slow decay started. It is also possible the polytheistic vs. monotheistic beliefs also undermined the very basis of the Hindu as well as the Jain religions. The leadership which was tentatively held by the religious leaders was also eroding rapidly. In my opinion, that period (1300A.D. to 1400 A.D.) is the beginning of the silent period.

3. The Colonial Rule (1700 A.D. to 1950 A.D.)

The interaction with Islamic mathematics and the Moslem rule was overshadowed by the European colonization. In the 18 to 20th centuries,

The previous 5000 years of Indian greatness in mathematics was often dismissed as a moribund interval of intellectual stagnation (Ref. 6) or decay for India. This opinion had its convenience for some European imperialists who wanted to argue foreign domination was helping to advance out of its "dark ages" (Ref. 6). In the words of a historian (Ref.7), Islam was largely seen to have been destructive of its remnants of the old Indian civilization and the British rule had done a lot to reinvigorate that old society. The British rule of over 200 years did bring about some changes in the Indian society and culture but they purposely did not touch the core of the Hindu society. It was Lord Elphinstone who advised the British Government not to touch the very essence of either the Hindu or the Moslem societies but to make friends with them by bringing in the British language so that would be helpful for the British Crown to maintain its hold on the Indian continent. That is the main reason English as a language was made compulsory for the Indians to learn so they can make very good civil servants to serve the British government. This was a very clever ploy employed by the Government, British scholars, officials and polemicists. I did not come across any reference where the British purposely planned to change or destroy the tenets of the Hindu society. But the emergence of the modern society made a lasting impression on the rather old Indian way of learning and that also continued the decay of the older civilization. There is so much written about the effect of the British rule of over 200 years, I do not want to add any more (Ref. 7&8).

Conclusions

I have listed three main reasons for the silent era or the demise of the greatness of the Indian mathematics from 1600 to the present day. There may be more reasons but these three are the major ones. I personally attribute the cause of the demise of the failure of the Indian

Society and to a far less extent to the other two. The two foreign invaders did not cause the fundamental change in the "core" system of the Hindu society. There was a systemic change from 4000B.C.onwards. It is very true that the 14th century works of Bhaskara 2 retained the canonical status in India for centuries. But as a result of combination of making it vernacular, colonial rule, Islamic invasion and the colonial rule, the academic tradition of Sanskrit mathematical science was essentially extinct in the last few hundred years.

There were major defects in the old Hindu society. The group of young learners who were full of devotion, loyalty, obedience and family traditions had slowly disappeared and was never replaced. The primary reason may be the original ideas were not fully understood and as generations went by, the halo was disappearing. The question of what Indian mathematics was fundamentally about which made it a coherent intellectual discipline in the universe of Sanskrit learning has been partially explored. The Indians did not understand or analyze the reasons what the early mathematicians were doing and why. As I stated earlier, I went through 30 articles and books, yet I did not come across any single Indian mathematical historian analyze the Silent Era. I consider that inexcusable. All these historians wrote about the glory of the mathematics repeatedly without adding anything new. Even I became a part of that group. Perhaps; it is easier to praise glories then to analyze the problem and to offer self-criticism. The only critical assessment I came across were from the scholars from the Edinburgh Society of Mathematics and the Royal Society of Mathematics. The subject of the Silent Era or the Demise of the greatness of Indian mathematics is a vast subject and hopefully, will be explored in the years to come. But I believe, the era of the greatness of the Indian mathematics is gone forever and may never be revived.

A Chronology of Eminent Indian Mathematicians

- Baudhayana (700 B.C.)
- Apastamba (600 B.C.)
- Katakana (500 B.C.)
- Masqat (1500B.C.)
- Aryabhata (476-550)

- Varahamihira (505-558)
- Brahmagupta (598-670)
- Covina swami (800-850)
- Mohair (850)
- Pruthudakaswami (850)
- Sridhar (900)
- Manual (930)
- Aryabhata2 (950)
- Prashastdhara (958)
- Halayudha (975)
- Jayadeva (1000)
- Seriatim (1039)
- Hem Chandra Sure (1089)
- Bjhaskara 2 (1114-1185)
- Canadian (1205)
- Mohave of Sangamagramma (1350-1425)
- Mahayana Pundit (1350)
- Parameswara(1360-1455)
- Mylanta Somayaji (1455-1555)
- Ankara Varian (1500-1560)
- Mahayana (1500-1675)
- Jyasthdeva (1550)
- Acute Disparate (1550-1621)
- Pitman Somayaji (1660-1740)
- Jacanas Pundit (1700)
- Ankara Varian (1800)

References

1. Joseph, G.G. (2000) The Crest of the Peacock, non – European roots of Mathematics.
   Princeton University Press
2. Gupta, R.C., (1990), the chronic problem of ancient Indian Chronology Ganita-Bharati, 12, 17-26.

3. P. Rushed, (1994), The development of Arabic Mathematics and Western Phenomenon, Netherlands, Clawer Academic Publishers.
4. Poker, Kim, (2009). Mathematics in India, Princeton University press.
5. Babul, C.T, (2006) Counting in Tamil, making texts from arithmetic in colonial Madras – presented at the Asian Society 2006.
6. Wilkinson, Lancelot (1834), On the use of the Sid hanta in the work of native education — Journal of the Asiatic Society of Bengal 3, 1834, 504-519.
7. Arnold, Danny, 2000 – Science and technology in colonial India, Cambridge University Press, 20.
8. Pollock, Sheldon (2001) the death of Sanskrit, comparative studies in history43.2, 2001, 392-426.

Chapter - 8

Intelligence Explosions in India Part One

The term "Intelligence Explosion" was invented by the eminent mathematician I.J. Good and the core idea was to invent brain-computer interfaces that can substantially augment human intelligence. I am deviating from this core idea and rely more on human intelligence which is the source of all technologies. So if technology improves intelligence that closes the loop and it produces a runaway positive feedback cycle. The purest case of this is a genuine artificial intelligence becoming smarter and then rewriting its own source code again. I have taken the liberty of conceiving an age of accelerated technological progress in two different periods in the Indian History. The early Indians used Intelligence as a Trump Card as a species. It is the human superpower and was widely used to improve existing conditions and literary awareness beyond anyone understands. In Part one, I will discuss the explosion that occurred in ancient India about 1500-200 B.C. In Part Two, I will discuss the events in about 1550-1750 A.D. before the colonial expansion in India. I believe India is the only country in the world to overcome the disasters to revive vigorously. Then came the second explosion and it died a slow demise.

I want to caution my readers this is my hypothesis based on my understanding of the magnitude and the excellence of the Indian accomplishments and I sincerely hope the future archaeologists will prove me correct because new evidences are being established.

Many factors played key roles in this period

1. Rapid and useful development of Mathematics
2. Widespread use of Sanskrit as a language after Panini
3. Tremendous advances in astronomy
4. Widespread use of trade via oceans and by the Silk Road.
5. Development of civil engineering in building temples, Roads, water distribution in cities etc.
6. High literacy rate and peaceful existence free of foreign attacks.
7. The pace of civilized shifted from Harrapa and Mohenjo Daro to the North Indian plains.

Let us go briefly in each section

1. **Mathematics**: It is without doubt mathematics today owes a huge debt to the outstanding contributions made by Indian mathematicians especially in the period from 1500 to 500 B.C. What is quite surprising is that there has been reluctance to recognize this. We shall look briefly at the development of the place-value decimal system of numbers and Indian numerals. Mathematicians began describing Geometry contained in the Sulbasustras but research has shown that the essential of this geometry was older being contained in the Altar construction of various temples.

We also know that the Harrapans had adopted a uniform system of weights and measures. An analysis of the weights discovered suggests that they belong to two series of both being Decimal in nature with each Decimal number multiplied and divided by two, giving for the main series of 0.05, 0.1, 0.2, 0.5, 1.2, 5, 10, 20, 30, 50, 100, 200, and 500. The next mathematics of importance was associated with the religious texts. It consisted of Sulbasutras which were appendices to the Vedas giving rules for constructing temples, and other edifices. The main Sulbasutras were composed by Baudhayana (about 800 B.C.), Manava (750 B.C.), Apastamba (600 B.C.) and Katyana (about 200 B.C.). These scholars were priests and not mathematicians in the modern sense. The texts are in their names but nobody knows who wrote these precious books.

There is another scholar who again was not a mathematician but lived around this period. That was Panini who achieved remarkable results in his studies of Sanskrit Grammar. Now you may ask what Sanskrit grammar has to do with mathematics. It certainly has something to with modern theoretical Computer Science, for a mathematician will recognize just how modern some of Panini's ideas are. Before the end of the period of the Sulbasutras, around the moddle of 550 B.C., the Brahmi numerals began to appear: 1, 2, 3, 4, 5, 6, 7, 8, 9. This is the first time in the history, Modern Numerals invented in India were extensively used in the world. What a revolution. It was equally impressive progress like the modern computers.

Jain Mathematics

The most impressive theory of numbers, arithmetical operations, geometry, operations with fractions, single equations, cubic equations, quadratic equations and various permutations and combinations. More surprisingly, the Jains developed the theory of Infinite containing different levels of Infinity, an understanding of Indices, and logarithms to the base **2.** ***Jain Mathematicsthis Truly Was An Explosion In Mathematics The World Had Ever Seen.***

If the Vedic religion gave rise to the study of Mathematics, the Jain mathematics gave a tremendous rise to the study of Astronomy. It was this science which required very accurate measurements and information about the planets and other heavenly bodies. Religion also played a very important role in the development of Astronomy combined with mathematics.

According to historians, the Hindu astronomers did not possess a general method of solving problems in Spherical Astronomy unlike the Greeks who developed following method of Ptolemy. But by means of suitable construction within the sphere, they were able to reduce many of their problems to comparison of right angled plane triangles. In addition to this device, they used the Quadratic Equations developed by Aryabhata and Bhaskara Two. This was the beginning of the Modern Astronomy as much as I know. Guess what? Nobody gave them any Credit. Everybody knows about Galileo. I can write far more but to bring this section to a close, I must state that the Development

Of Indian Mathematics was one of the most significant developments that appeared on this planet and what an Explosion of Ideas that was.

2. The Development Of Sanskrit As A Language: The mentality of Mankind and the language created each other. If we like to assume the rise of the language as a given fact, then it is not going too far to say that the souls of men and women are the gifts from language to mankind. The account for the sixth day should be written: **He gave them speech, and they became souls** Alfred North Whitehead and Lord Bertrand Russell in Modes of Thought.

This quote may have created in the readers as many different responses as there are readers. One may perceive it as a noble and inspiring truth. Perhaps we should recreate North and Russell's quote and say "He gave speech and they became souls and in turn some of them gave souls to all creatures, to all life." All this is not to in any way invalidate the sanctity and perfection of creation but only to point out that we have greatly underestimated the sacred power of the language. When the power of language to create and discover life is recognized, language becomes sacred. In Ancient India, the language was held in this regard. There is a lot of evidence that the ancient Indian scientists of language were acutely aware of the function of the language as a tool for exploring and understanding life, and in the process of using language with greater and greater rig our discovered Sanskrit or the "PERFECT LANGUAGE".

In Ancient India, the intention to discover the TRUTH was so consuming, that in the process, they discovered perhaps the most perfect tool for fulfilling such a search that the World has ever known - the Sanskrit Language. Without language, the civilization could not survive. On the other hand, to the degree that language becomes sophisticated and accurate in describing the subtlety and complexity of human life, we gain power and effectiveness in meeting its challenges.

Relevant to this, there has recently been an astounding discovery made at NASA research Center. The following quote is from an article which appeared in AI (Artificial Intelligence)

Magazine in 1985

In the past 20 years, much time, effort and money has been

expended on designing an in ambiguous representation of natural language to make them accessible to computer processing. These efforts have centered around creating schemata designed to parallel logical relations with relations expressed by the syntax and semantics of the natural languages, which are clearly cumbersome and ambiguous in their function as vehicles is a widespread belief that natural languages are unsuitable for the transmission of many ideas that artificial language can render with great precision and mathematical rigor.

But this dichotomy is a false one. There is at least one language, SANSKRIT, which for the duration of almost 2000 years was a living spoken language with a considerable literature of its own. Besides works of literary value, there was a long philosophical and grammatical tradition that has continued to exist with undiminished vigor until the present century. Sanskrit can be reckoned not only in essence but in the form with current work in ARTIFICIAL INTELLIGENCE (AI).

Did the ancient Indians know about the power of Sanskrit as AI language? A brief history of Sanskrit: The origin of the Sanskrit language can be accredited to the VEDIC society. Vedic Sanskrit is believed to date back to 2000 B.C. when knowledge was handed down verbally through generations.

About 550 B.C., a Hindu grammarian by the name of Panini had formally recorded the rules of Sanskrit Grammar. This is known as ASHTADHYAYI. It contains 8 chapters, each divided into four sections or “Padas”. It characterizes the difference between the language of the sacred texts and that of the common street language (rules of Sanskrit morphology have been set out, much in the way of a mathematical function, to define the basic elements of the language including sentence structure, vowels, nouns and verbs. Panini’s original work is still used in the teaching of Sanskrit today. Classical Sanskrit as opposed to its more archaic ancestor Vedic Sanskrit was in the height in the centuries A.D.

3. Astronomy

Calendars of the world have usually been set by the Sun and the Moon (measuring the day, month and year) and were important to the agricultural societies, in which the harvest depended on planting at the correct time of the year. There are astronomical references of chronological significance in the Vedic notices mark the beginning and the end of the year of the Vernal equinox in Orion. This was in about 1500 B.C. Yajnavalkya (perhaps in 1400 B.C.) described the motions of the Sun and the Moon in his book Shatapatha Brahmana and also advanced a 95 year old cycle to synchronize the motions of the Sun and The Moon. In Sanskrit, the science of astronomy is called Khagola-Shastra. The word Khagola perhaps is derived from the famous astronomical laboratory at the University of Nalanda which was called Khagola. It was at Khagola that the world famous Indian astronomer, Aryabhatta studied and extended the subject. Around 500 B.C., Aryabhatta presented a mathematical system that took Earth to spin on its axis and considered the motions of the planets with respect to the Sun. He also made accurate calculations of the Earth's circumference, Diameter, and how the lunar eclipse and the solar eclipse occur for the first time. He gave the radius of the planetary orbits in terms of the radius of the Earth/Sun as essentially their periods of rotation around the Sun. He was also the earliest to discover that the orbits of the planets around the Sun are Ellipses.

The lack of a telescope hindered further advancement of ancient Indian astronomy. Though it should be admitted that with the unaided observations and calculations with crude instruments, the astronomers in Ancient India were able to arrive at precise measurements. There is an old Sanskrit Sloka (couplet) which is:

"Sarva Dishanaam, Surya, Surya, Surya"

This couplet means that there are Suns in all directions. Also, it describes the night sky as full of Suns, indicates that in ancient times Indian astronomers had arrived at the important discovery that the stars visible at night are similar to the Sun visible during the day. In other words, the Sun is also a Star, though the nearest one.There is so much to write on this subject and I will cover it in another article. Suffice to state; the astronomical information existed long before the Greek astronomers developed it. I personally have no words to describe the fantastic developments in astronomy in ancient India. It truly is a rare accomplishment in the good period of 1500-500 B.C.

4. Other Developments

There were other accomplishments in civil engineering, aero planes building, developments of missiles and the construction of roads in big cities and other subjects are not covered in this article because the dates vary all over the board and stories are not easy to substantiate. Here, we want a substantial archaeological work to support some findings.

Conclusions

Indian wisdom and Western materialism epitomizes the quest of eternal truth by Homo sapiens. Through millennia B.C., indigenous Indian wisdom extensively spread to other countries. During this period especially during 1500-500 B.C., the influx and interaction of different political, religious, ethnic and linguistic people built a colorful mosaic of Culture and Tradition on its foundation. As a student of history, I have never read anywhere anything coming close to the Indian accomplishments. Unfortunately, the luster of Indian Wisdom got tarnished, occluded and somewhat destroyed after this period. There are many reason for this, mainly India's unguarded boundaries on the Northern side were penetrated by the tribes and the people who were too complacent to care about their country. Fortunately, this period lasted for about 500 years and was revived in about 1550 A.D. I will cover this in Part Two.

Chapter - 9

Intelligence Explosions in India Part Two

Introduction

In Part 1, we discussed the subject in the Time Period of 1500 - 500 B.C. Now, in Part 2, we will go into the time period of 1500 -1750 A.D. I believe these two periods were critical when the Intelligence Explosions occurred in various spheres of the country's life and changed the course for good.

The two periods mentioned earlier did show what the country is capable of achieving in every sphere of the country's life. When you go past these periods, you suddenly come across India's ills which, I believe, were primarily self-imposed derived from poor strategic thinking, lack of self-confidence and a tendency towards fratricide.

The Period from 1500-1750 A.D.

Before we go in detail of this period, I want to emphasize that in my opinion, the growth of Indian mathematics, astronomy and other science subject from the ancient days rested mainly on the development of Sanskrit as the principal driving force. All other subjects followed the progress of Sanskrit. Classical Sanskrit literature in all genres tends to be very conscious of the languages phonetic and grammatical structure. Mathematical texts in particular may make use of the Sanskrit alphabet, for verse friendly forms of number representation, or construct syllabic abbreviations for mathematical quantities, or adapt grammatical technical terms as mathematical ones. I hope my readers will agree with me about the major role of Sanskrit in development of the Indian advancement from ancient India.

Individuals, Families and School

Today, we have a fuller historical picture of some prominent mathematicians after about 1500 A.D. than ever before. The first thing that one notices about Indian scholars of the Sanskrit tradition at this time period is that there are many more of them then before. Readers have to remember that manuscripts were still copied by hand.

A few examples of "Scientific Schools" or family traditions in particular localities during this period illustrate the kind of contextual information available.

1.Parthapura -15th century - Parthapura, a small town on the Godavari River identified with modern Pathri, about 100 kilometers from Aurangabad in Maharashtra was a regional center of astronomical and mathematical activities. The earliest known ancestor was Ganesa born in1507 .He developed the astronomical works of Karana and Kosthaka, the entire school was known to have written Jytotisa works.

2.Varanasi - 16 and 17th centuries. The greatest metropolis of Sanskrit learning at this time was the city of Varanasi also known as Benares or Kashi .The city was a magnet for scholars from all over the country, some of them received funding from their local rulers to study and work there. Ganesa's student Divakara from the Parthapura region moved to Varanasi after completing his studies in Nandigrama.

3. Courts in Delhi and Other Places: Well-known astronomers under Shah Jahan, the Emperor and other mathematicians developed advanced formulae in algebra, calculus, geometry and trigonometry.

Contacts with Europe

In the early 17th century, the British East India Company obtained permission from the Mughal Emperor, Jehangir to establish trading centers on the India's eastern coast, at Calcutta and Madras. The Portuguese and the British were followed by the French, the Dutch and the Danes mostly in southern and eastern India. During the course of these developments, Indians and Europeans became acquainted to some extent with each other's languages and cultures, and in the process, transmitted knowledge about their respective systems of mathematical sciences. I have covered a good deal of this interchange in my earlier articles and will not repeat it here.

The Role of Sanskrit

The two centuries before European colonialism established itself decisively in the Indian sub-continent, constitute one of the most innovative eras of Sanskrit literature studies, tremendous advancement in mathematics, astronomy and other subjects. Thinkers began to work across disciplines far more intensively than ever before, to produce new formulations of old problems, to employ strikingly new discursive idiom in what were genres of scholarly writing. Concurrent with the spread of European power in the mid-eighteenth century, however, this dynamism began to diminish. By the end of the Century, the tradition of Sanskrit systematic thought which for two millennium or more constituted one of the most remarkable cultural formation in the World history—had more or less vanished as a force in shaping the Indian intellectual life to be replaced by other kinds of knowledge based on different principles of knowing and acting in the world.

These two phases are the core issues of this research project

The nature of the " Knowledge System" or scholarly disciplines in India just before the beginning of the Colonial rule and the fact of their decline in the face of the new knowledge or the grounds of knowledge and social regime of European modernity. At the present time, a new project has been undertaken to link four tasks: inventory the intellectual production in seven disciplines during this period; collect unpublished manuscripts and documents from archives in India, collect bibliographical and photographic database derived from many sources. I hope this book will be published in the very near future to offer an account of the Sanskrit disciplines and the intellectuals who produced them at the moment both were about to be transformed utterly.

To date, nobody understands how to account for what appears to have been the explosion of intellectual production in Sanskrit in the

17th century. There are no acceptable accounts of the scholarly work for individual disciplines, let alone across them; or the key contributors of the major thinkers. Although political-economic changes of the sort found in Bengal at the time are sometimes identified as the critical factor, the decline in the quantity and quality of Sanskrit scholarly production in some places seems to have begun before then, and elsewhere does not set in until later. Counter-tendencies such as the attempt by the Peshwas in mid -18th century Maharashtra to revive Sanskrit scholarship need careful assessment. Other casual factors of a social nature, such as the diminishing influence of the courtly society, or the loss of vitality of the Sanskrit educational system, are more difficult to evaluate, since so little sound scholarship is available. The transformed political landscape in South India, Thanjavur was taken by Wellesley in 1799; in the North, Varanasi was ceded to the British in 1803; in the West, the Peshwas of Maharashtra were defeated in the course of the following decade clearly needs to be taken into consideration. We have to remember that the historiography of the non-Mughal politics is quite thin and needs a lot of work to get a better picture.

Most pertinent is the intellectual sphere itself, and the kinds of exchange that took place within and across the knowledge system. But here, too, we are pretty much in the dark. Direct confrontation between Indian and European learning was as rare as that between Sanskrit and Persian scholarships during the previous three centuries. In other words, the confrontation was one sided : As modernizing Europe attacked vociferously, Sanskrit retreated in silence; no Shastri (teacher) even bothered to answer the critique, made so painfully explicit by Macaulay and his compatriots. Later thinkers such as Ram Mohan Roy did respond, it was from an already colonized, even westernized perspective. Forms of Sanskrit science without close analogy in the West, such as language analysis disappeared as creative modes of thought in the face of what were vaguely comparable European forms.

It is no easy matter, then, to grasp the reasons at the level of individual philosophical or scientific concept why Sanskrit knowledge at the end of the 18th century lost the vitality and confidence that had marked it in the preceding two centuries.

I believe there are Sanskrit texts in philosophy, literary theory, astral sciences, and the like in large quantities and which, form the primary data to investigate and research in a new project as to the reasons for sudden eclipse of the Sanskrit language.

Yet, it was at this historical juncture that a great divergence between the two traditions occurred, as a set of important changes in the production and dissemination of knowledge began to manifest them as late-renaissance of knowledge and early enlightened Europe. This is a long familiar list, which includes new procedures in method, (empiricism), new kinds of conceptualization (Quantification), new attitudes towards the past (critical rationalism), new communicative codes, new institutional sites such as royal academy, new publication journals and most important is the public awareness. As I understand, nothing of this type occurred in India from the end of the 16th century. There was no Bengali Descartes, nor Maharashtrian Bacon or Hindi Shakespeare to talk about. The end result was unlike the language of learning, the material and social composition of the Sanskrit language remained largely unchanged.

Conclusions

It is essential to point out that Sanskrit was the dominant force in the intellectual world for over 3000 years. I am certain that the early Sanskrit intellectuals were attempting to formulate the society with vast boundaries but in a disciplined manner. They succeeded beyond any imagination in the beginning with vast spread of mathematics, astronomy and other sciences. This success went on until the beginning of 100 A.D. Then the Muslim invaders and the Mughal Empire obliterated the early success with Sanskrit. The discipline that was built was gone. The society was without any guidance. This went on until the beginning of the 15th century and the Sanskrit era was revived for two centuries. I believe, today, we are in the midst of the continuing crisis where there is no discipline in the society .We are copying the American success with the money part playing a major role without any deep foundation. What the country needs is a very rigid disciplined structure with emphasis on fundamental knowledge. Unless the country undergoes this change, the crisis will continue indefinitely.

Other Articles On Mathematics